HEARTS OF DARKNESS

◆

THE RADICAL IMAGINATION SERIES
Edited by Henry A. Giroux and Stanley Aronowitz

Now Available

Beyond the Spectacle of Terrorism: Global Uncertainty and the Challenge of the New Media
  by Henry A. Giroux

Hearts of Darkness: Torturing Children in the War on Terror
  by Henry A. Giroux

Politics After Hope: Obama and the Crisis of Youth, Race, and Democracy
  by Henry A. Giroux

Forthcoming

A Future for the American Left
  by Stanley Aronowitz

Afromodernity: How Europe Is Evolving toward Africa
  by Jean Comaroff and John L. Comaroff

HEARTS OF DARKNESS
TORTURING CHILDREN
IN THE WAR ON TERROR

HENRY A. GIROUX

Paradigm Publishers
Boulder • London

Copyright © 2010 Paradigm Publishers

Published in the United States by Paradigm Publishers, 2845 Wilderness Place, Suite 200, Boulder, CO 80301 USA.

Paradigm Publishers is the trade name of Birkenkamp & Company, LLC, Dean Birkenkamp, President and Publisher.

Library of Congress Cataloging-in-Publication Data

Giroux, Henry A.
  Hearts of darkness : torturing children in the war on terror / Henry A. Giroux.
     p. cm. — (The radical imagination series)
  Includes bibliographical references and index.
  ISBN 978-1-59451-825-6 (alk. paper)
  ISBN 978-1-59451-826-3 (pbk. : alk. paper)
  1. Children and war—United States. 2. Torture—Government policy—United States. 3. War on Terrorism, 2001–2009.
I. Title.
  HQ784.W3G57 2010
  362.87—dc22
                                                            2010000838

Printed and bound in the United States of America on acid-free paper that meets the standards of the American National Standard for Permanence of Paper for Printed Library Materials.

Designed and Typeset by Straight Creek Bookmakers.

14 13 12 11 10   1 2 3 4 5

For Susan, my muse

And for Stanley Aronowitz and Howard Zinn, whose moral
courage is matched by their political wisdom

Contents

◇

Foreword

As *Hearts of Darkness* makes clear, torture is a cancer within an open society. It empowers a class of sadists and killers who seek greater and greater latitude to abuse helpless and often innocent victims. These sadists and killers soon make no distinction between internal and external enemies. They do not distinguish, as Henry Giroux points out, between children and adults. All human beings, even children, become dehumanized objects that are seen as embodying an external evil that must be eradicated. Torturers, intoxicated with the power to play god, swiftly fall prey to their bizarre conspiracy theories and misconceptions. The larger the fantasies, the more brutal and expansive are the methods used to extract useless and absurd fragments of information that sustain these fantasies. Those who use torture descend to the level of beasts. And the pact made between torturers and the states that routinely use torture builds terrifying international bonds of depravity and violence that mock democratic institutions. The use of torture transforms crimes into an acceptable method of law enforcement. It transforms the innocent into the guilty. It transforms a democracy into a gulag. Torture robs us of the capacity for empathy and compassion, of mutual respect, and of the rule of law, all of which are vital to the maintenance of a civil society. As soon as a civilization permits torture, it begins to die.

When an intelligence service depends on torture to extract information, it is broken. Torture is the least efficient way to gain information and is always employed by those who are as desperate as they are blind. The Central Intelligence Agency (CIA) has relied on intelligence based on torture in prisons in Uzbekistan, a place where practices include raping suspects with broken bottles and *boiling them alive,* according to Craig Murray, a former British ambassador to Uzbekistan. Suspects were sent there by the CIA as part of the extraordinary rendition program. But Uzbekistan is only one country among many despotic backwaters that have become America's allies in the "war on terror" because they also have done away with legal impediments to abuse. Only 1 percent of the prisoners held offshore by the United States are held at Guantánamo; the rest end up in the hands of a worldwide network of torturers in countries such as Uzbekistan.

"I'm talking of people being raped with broken bottles," Murray said. "I'm talking of people having their children tortured in front of them until they sign a confession. I'm talking of people being boiled alive. And the intelligence from these torture sessions was being received by the CIA, and was being passed on."[1]

Suspects in Uzbekistan's torture centers "were being told to confess to membership in Al Qaeda. They were told to confess they'd been in training camps in Afghanistan. They were told to confess they had met Osama bin Laden in person. And the CIA intelligence constantly echoed these themes."

"I was absolutely stunned—it changed my whole world view in an instant—to be told that London knew [the intelligence] coming from torture, that it was not illegal because our legal advisers had decided that under the United Nations convention against torture, it is not illegal to obtain or use intelligence gained from torture as long as we didn't do the torture ourselves," Murray said.

But in the United States, the government no longer relies, as it did during the Cold War, exclusively on third parties to do the torturing for it. The attacks of 9/11 freed U.S. authorities from moral and legal constraints. President Barack Obama not only continues to permit the torture authorized by George W. Bush but has gone on to embrace his predecessor's radical secrecy laws. Obama too oversees black sites where people, many of whom are innocent and never charged with a crime, vanish from outside view and are subjected to terrible human cruelty. The documents released from the International Committee of the Red Cross, from the U.S. Justice Department's Office of Legal Council (OLC), and from the House Armed Services Committee illustrate that torture is a tactic routinely employed by the CIA and the U.S. military. Waterboarding may be proscribed, but many other forms of torture continue, including prolonged isolation, solitary confinement, sleep and sensory deprivation, force-feeding, and an emotional technique called "fear up," which involves terrifying prisoners into a state of "learned helplessness." Torture is masked under complex and nuanced legalities that resemble the convoluted edicts issued by the Jesuits to "legalize" the torture techniques employed in the Inquisition. What is the allowable incline for a waterboard? How many calories will suffice to avoid starvation? Which insects are permitted to be used in driving a man insane? These subtle questions of degree have replaced questions of ethics.

If those detained in American black sites go on hunger strikes, they are strapped to chairs and food is forced down their throats. Force-feeding, which happens routinely in American detention centers, is defended as a humanitarian gesture to keep prisoners alive. Article 3 of the Geneva Convention, however, forbids "humiliating and degrading treatment," which includes force-feeding. Hernán Reyes, in a 1998 policy review for the International Committee of the Red Cross, wrote: "Doctors should never be party to actual coercive feeding, with prisoners being tied down and intravenous drips or oesophageal tubes being forced into them. Such actions can be considered a form of torture, and under no circumstances should doctors participate in them, on the pretext of 'saving the hunger striker's life.'"

The prisoners who are force-fed are not facing death. The force-feedings begin as soon as a prisoner starts a hunger strike. The process entails military guards strapping prisoners to restraint chairs, usually for several hours at a time, where they must often sit covered in their own vomit. They endure force-feeding until they agree to end the hunger strike. "Dietary manipulation," as force-feeding is now labeled, is lauded as an effective "conditioning technique" to help gather "intelligence." It has become another tool used to break prisoners.

Red Cross interviews acquired by Mark Danner and published in the *New York Review of Books* illustrate the trauma of dietary manipulation, as this example shows:

> During the first two weeks I did not receive any food. I was only given Ensure and water to drink. A guard would come and hold the bottle for me while I drank.... During the first month I was not provided with any food apart from on two occasions as a reward for perceived cooperation. I was given Ensure to drink every 4 hours. If I refused to drink then my mouth was forced open by the guard and it was poured down my throat by force.... I was transferred to a chair where I was kept, shackled by [the] hands and feet [and] given no solid food during the first two or three weeks, while sitting on the chair. I was only given Ensure and water to drink. At first the Ensure made me vomit, but this became less with time.

Ahmed Ghappour, an attorney with the human rights group Reprieve, which represents thirty-one detainees at Guantánamo, told Reuters that prison officials were "over-force-feeding" hunger strikers, who were suffering from diarrhea as they sat tied to their chairs. He charged that prison officials were lacing the nutrient shakes with laxatives. "According to my clients, there has been a ramping up in abuse since President Obama was inaugurated," Ghappour said, speculating that guards there wanted to "get their kicks in" before the camp closed.

David Remes, an attorney who represents fifteen detainees at Guantánamo, wrote in a petition to the U.S. District Court for the District of Columbia that when one of his clients, Farhan Abdul Latif, has the nasogastric tube inserted into his body, it "is threaded though his nostril into his stomach" and "feels like a nail going into his nostril, and like a knife going down his throat." Some of the striking detainees now keep their feeding tubes in their noses even when not being force-fed to avoid having the tubes painfully reinserted. Latif has in recent months resorted to covering himself with his own excrement in order "to avoid force-feeding and ... when he was finally force-fed, the tube was inserted through the excrement covering his nostrils."

Latif, who is now being held in Guantánamo's "Behavioral Health Unit," appears, like many detainees, to have been broken by his confinement. Remes said that his client has made several suicide attempts. Latif attempted at one point to kill himself in his lawyer's presence. "Without my noticing, he chipped off a piece of stiff veneer from the underside of the table and used it to saw into a vein in his left wrist," Remes said. "As he sawed, he drained his blood into a plastic container I had brought and, shortly before our time was up, he hurled the blood at me from the container. It must have been a good deal of blood because I was drenched from the top of my head to my knees."

The following excerpt is part of the sworn statement of an interpreter at the Kandahar detention facility in Afghanistan. The handwritten document is dated February 13, 2002:

I am writing this in response to events that I witnessed while performing my duties as an interrogator with the Task Force 202 JIF. Specialist [blank] and I were conducting an interrogation of military prisoner number [blank] on 3 January, 2002. Special Forces personnel had been visiting the booth area previously and helping out by giving information that they had from their raids. [Blank] and I took a break to regroup and check our notes. I was the translator. While we were out of the booth, several Special Forces members entered the booth. At the time I did not think anything of it, and thought they were just observing him based on previous experiences with their people. This was a different group of [Special Forces] people I hadn't seen before. [Blank] and I finished the break and went back to continue the interrogation. When we entered the booth, we found the Special Forces members all crouched around the prisoner. They were blowing cigarette smoke in his face. The prisoner was extremely upset. It took a long time to calm him down and find out what had happened. The prisoner was visibly shaken and crying. [Blank] immediately told them to get out and not to come back anywhere near anyone that we were talking to. I could tell something was wrong. The prisoner was extremely upset. He said that they had hit him, told him that he was going to die, blew smoke in his face, and had shocked him with some kind of device. He used the term "electricity."

I immediately notified our Non-Commissioned Officer in Charge of what had happened.

I was very upset that such a thing could happen. I take my job and responsibilities as an interrogator and as a human being very seriously. I understand the importance of the Geneva Convention and what it represents. If I don't honor it, what right do I have to expect any other military to do so?

Abu Zubaydah gave a firsthand account of his interrogation in a secret CIA prison. His testimony is included in a report by the International Committee of the Red Cross about the treatment of detainees in U.S. custody:

About two and a half or three months after I arrived in this place, the interrogation began again, but with more intensity than before. Then the real torturing started. Two black wooden boxes were brought into the room outside my cell. One was tall, slightly higher than me and narrow, measuring perhaps 1 meter by three-quarters of a meter and 2 meters in height. The other was shorter, perhaps only 1 meter in height. I was taken out of my cell and one of the interrogators wrapped a towel around my neck, they then used it to swing me around and smash me repeatedly against the hard walls of the room. I was also repeatedly slapped in the face. As I was still shackled, the pushing and pulling around meant that the shackles pulled painfully on my ankles. I was then put into the tall box for what I think was about one and a half to two hours. The box was totally black on the inside as well as the outside. It had a bucket inside to use as a toilet and had water to drink provided in a bottle.... It was difficult to breathe. When I was let out of the box I saw that one of the walls of the room had been covered with plywood sheeting. From now on it was against this wall that I was then smashed with the towel around my neck. I think that the plywood was there to provide some absorption of the impact of my body. The interrogators realized that smashing me against the hard wall would probably quickly result in physical injury. During these torture sessions many guards were present, plus two interrogators who did the actual beating still asking questions, while the main interrogator left to return when the beating was over. After the beating I was then placed in the small box.... The wound on my leg began to open and started to bleed. I don't know how long I remained in the small box, I think I may have slept or maybe fainted.... [Later, I was taken from the box] and put on what looked like a hospital bed, and strapped down very tightly with belts. A black cloth was then placed over my face and the interrogators [poured] water on the cloth so that I could not breathe.... The same torture [was] carried out again.... I thought I was going to die.... I was then placed again in the tall box ... then taken out ... and smashed into the wall.... This went on for approximately one week. During this time the whole procedure was repeated five times. On each occasion, apart from one, I was suffocated once or twice and was put in the vertical position on the bed in between. On one occasion the suffocation was repeated three times. I vomited each time I was put in the vertical position between the suffocation. During that week I was not given any solid food, I was only given Ensure to drink. My head and beard were shaved every day. I collapsed and lost consciousness on several occasions. Eventually the torture was stopped by the intervention of the doctor. I was told during this period that I was one of the first to receive these interrogation techniques, so no rules applied. It felt like they were experimenting and trying out techniques to be used later on other people.

The "Interrogation Log of Detainee 063," an eighty-three-page document, details minute by minute the seven-week interrogation of Mohammed al-Qahtani, which took place from November 2002 to January 2003 at Camp X-Ray, Guantánamo Bay, Cuba. It gives a close look into how prisoners are slowly broken and even driven insane through lack of sleep, isolation, and abuse over weeks and months in captivity.

Lt. Col. Darrel Vandeveld was the army reserve judge advocate and former lead prosecutor in the military commission case of Guantánamo detainee Mohammed Jawad. As Giroux points out in *Hearts of Darkness*, Vandeveld removed himself from the case on ethical grounds and submitted this sworn statement in support of Jawad's habeas petition, which was filed by the American Civil Liberties Union (ACLU):

> I, Darrel Vandeveld, declare as follows:
> I am a Lieutenant Colonel in the Judge Advocate General Corps. Since the September 2001 attacks, I have served in Bosnia, Africa, Iraq and Afghanistan. My awards include the Bronze Star Medal, the Iraqi Campaign Medal, and two Joint Meritorious Unit Awards.

Interrogation Log of Detainee 063

13 December 2002

0001: Upon entering the booth, lead played the call to prayer with a special alarm clock. Detainee was told, "this is no longer the call to prayer. You're not allowed to pray. This is the call to interrogation. So pay attention." Both lead and control participated in a "pride and ego down" approach. Control told detainee, "UBL has made a whore of Islam. Since you follow UBL, you also rape Islam." Control put a sign on detainee that had the Arabic word for coward written on it. Explained how the words liar, stupid, weak, and failure apply to detainee. Detainee showed very little emotion during the initial portion of the session, except for the occasional smug smile that was met with immediate taunts and ridicule from the interrogators.

0120: Lead ordered detainee to go to bathroom and walk for twenty minutes. Refused water. Corpsman checked his vital signs and stated he was fine. Both interrogators continued with the "futility" and "pride and ego down" approaches. On occasion when the detainee began to drift off into sleep, lead dripped a couple of drops of water on detainee's head to keep him awake. Detainee jerked violently in his chair each time.

0240: After a bathroom and walking break and detainee's refusal of water, the interrogators continued the aforementioned approaches. Detainee showed little response during this session. Detainee became increasingly tired and incoherent.

0320: Detainee received walking and bathroom break. Refused water. He then slept for one hour, followed by one hour in his chair listening to white noise.

continues

0530: Control showed detainee the banana rats and stated that they live better than he does. Lead asked detainee, "What do you think is going to happen to you? What would a judge do if he saw all the information that links you to Al-Qaida?" Detainee stated, "I'm not associated with Al-Qaida." After that statement, control read all circumstantial evidence collected against detainee. Detainee attempted to hide his emotions, but was clearly frightened when asked if the judge had enough evidence to convict him.

0700: Detainee walked, refused water, and allowed to begin four hour rest period.

1100: Detainee awakened and offered coffee—refused.

1115: Detainee taken to bathroom and walked 10 minutes. Offered water—refused. Interrogators began telling detainee how ungrateful and grumpy he was. In order to escalate the detainee's emotions, a mask was made from an MRE box with a smiley face on it and placed on the detainee's head for a few moments. A latex glove was inflated and labeled the "sissy slap" glove. This glove was touched to the detainee's face periodically after explaining the terminology to him. The mask was placed back on the detainee's head. While wearing the mask, the team began dance instruction with the detainee. The detainee became agitated and began shouting. The mask was removed and detainee was allowed to sit. Detainee shouted and addressed lead as "the oldest Christian here" and wanted to know why lead allowed the detainee to be treated this way.

1300: Detainee taken to bathroom and walked 10 minutes.

1320: Detainee offered food and water—refused. Detainee was unresponsive for remainder of session.

continues

Afghanistan/Taliban themes run for remainder of session.

1430: Detainee taken to bathroom and walked 10 minutes.

1500: Detainee offered water—refused.

1510: Corpsman changed bandages on ankles, checked vitals—O.K.

1530: Detainee taken to bathroom and walked 10 minutes.

1600: Corpsman checks vitals and starts IV. Detainee given three bags of IV.

1745: Detainee taken to bathroom and walked 10 minutes.

1800: Detainee was unresponsive.

1833: Detainee was allowed to sleep.

1925: The detainee was awakened by interrogation team. He was offered food and water but he refused.

1945: The interrogation team and detainee watched the video "Operation Enduring Freedom."

2120: Detainee was sent to the latrine. Offered water but he refused.

2200: Detainee exercised for good health and circulation. Medical representative took detainee's vital signs and removed the IV housing unit from the detainee's arm. The detainee's pulse rate was low (38) and his blood pressure was high (144/90). Detainee complained of having a boil on his left leg, just below his knee. The medical representative looked at the leg and phoned the doctor. The doctor instructed the corpsman to recheck the detainee's vitals in one hour.

continues

2300: Detainee refused water and food. He was taken to the latrine and exercised in order to assist in improving the detainee's vital signs.

2345: The medical representative rechecked the detainee's vital signs. The detainee's blood pressure had improved but it was still high (138/80) and his pulse rate had improved but it remained low (42). The corpsman called the doctor to provide an update and the doctor said operations could continue since there had been no significant change. It was noted that historically the detainee's pulse sometimes drops into the 40s in the evenings.

I offer this declaration in support of Mohammed Jawad's petition for habeas corpus.

I was the lead prosecutor assigned to the Military Commissions case against Mr. Jawad until my resignation in September 2008. Initially, the case appeared to be as simple as the street crimes I had prosecuted by the dozens in civilian life. But eventually I began to harbor serious doubts about the strength of the evidence.

Mr. Jawad was alleged to have thrown a grenade at U.S. troops, but the victims of the attack had not seen the attacker. At least three other Afghans had been arrested for the crime and had subsequently confessed, casting considerable doubt on the claim that Mr. Jawad was solely responsible for the attack. And I learned that the written statement characterized as Jawad's personal confession could not possibly have been written by him because Jawad was functionally illiterate and could not read or write. The statement was not even in his native language.

I also found evidence that Mr. Jawad had been badly mistreated by U.S. authorities both in Afghanistan and Guantanamo. Mr. Jawad's prison records referred to a suicide attempt, a suicide which he sought to accomplish by banging his head repeatedly against one of his cell walls. The records reflected 112 unexplained moves from cell to cell over a two week period, an average of eight moves per day for 14 days. Mr. Jawad had been subjected to a sleep deprivation program known as the "frequent flyer program."

I lack the words to express the heartsickness I experienced when I came to understand the pointless, purely gratuitous mistreatment of Mr. Jawad by my fellow soldiers.

It is my opinion, based on my extensive knowledge of the case, that there is no credible evidence or legal basis to justify Mr. Jawad's detention in U.S. custody or his prosecution by military commission. Holding Mr. Jawad for six years, with no resolution of his case and with no terminus in sight, is something beyond a travesty.

I have taken an oath to support and defend the Constitution of the United States and I remain confident that I have done so, spending over four of the past seven years away from my family, my home, my civilian occupation—all without any expectation of or desire for any reward greater than the knowledge that I have remained true to my word and have done my level best to rise to our Nation's defense in its time of need.

I did not "quit" the military commissions or resign; instead, I personally petitioned the Army's Judge Advocate General to allow me to serve the remaining six months of my two year voluntary obligation in Afghanistan or Iraq. In the exercise of his wisdom and discretion, he permitted me to be released from active duty. However, had I been returned to Afghanistan or Iraq, and had I encountered Mohammed Jawad in either of those hostile lands, where two of my friends have been killed in action and another one of my very best friends was terribly wounded, I have no doubt at all—*none*—that Mr. Jawad would pose no threat whatsoever to me, his former prosecutor and now-repentant persecutor.

Six years is long enough for a boy of sixteen to serve in virtual solitary confinement in a distant land, for reasons he may never fully understand. Mr. Jawad should be released to resume his life in a civil society, for his sake, and for our own sense of justice and perhaps to restore a measure of our basic humanity.

Torture, finally, takes lives. It implicates the United States in gratuitous acts of murder. The autopsy and death reports of detainees who died in U.S. custody in Iraq and Afghanistan provide another window into the physical brutality unleashed on people who have been deprived of legal representation or a trial. Here are a few such reports:

Autopsy Number: AO3-51. Date of Death: June 6th, 2003. Decedent is a ... 52 year old Iraqi Male, Civilian Detainee, who was found unresponsive outside in isolation at White-horse detainment facility.

This ... 52-year-old Male, [REDACTED] died as a result of asphyxia (lack of oxygen to the brain) due to strangulation. Additional findings at autopsy include blunt force injuries, predominantly recent bruises, on the torso and lower extremities. The abrasions encircling the left wrist are consistent with the use of restraints.

Cause of Death: Strangulation
Manner of Death: Homicide

Autopsy Number: ME 03-504.... Date of Death: November 4th, 2003. An Iraqi National, died while detained at the Abu Ghraib prison where he was held for interrogations by government agencies. Fractures of the ribs and a contusion of the left lung imply significant blunt force injuries of the thorax and likely resulted in impaired respiration.... Interviews taken from individuals present during the interrogation indicate that a hood was placed over the head and neck of the detainee. This likely resulted in further compromise of effective respiration.

Cause of Death: Blunt Force Injuries Complicated by Compromised Respiration
Manner of Death: Homicide

Autopsy Number: Me03-571.... Date of Death: November 26th, 2003. This Iraqi ... died while in U.S. custody. The details surrounding the circumstances at the time of death are classified.

Cause of Death: Asphyxia due to smothering and chest compression.

Manner of death: Homicide.

Death: April 5, 2004
Location: LSA Diamon
Questioned by NSWT, struggled/interrogated/died sleeping
Cause and Manner: Pending
Death: Jan. 1, 2004
Location: FOB Rifles
Questioned by "other government agency," gagged in standing restraint
Cause: Blunt force injuries & asphyxia
Manner of Death: Homicide

Death: Nov. 26, 2004
Location: FOB Tiger
Questioned by "military intelligence," died during interrogation
Cause: Asphyxia due to smothering & chest compression
Manner of Death: Homicide

Death: Nov. 4, 2003
Location: Abu Ghraib
Questioned by "other government agency" and NSWT; died during interrogation
Cause: Blunt force injury complicated by compromised respiration
Manner of Death: Homicide

Death: December 10, 2002
Location: Bagram, Afghanistan

Found unresponsive in cell
Cause: Blunt force injuries to lower extremities . . .
Manner of Death: Homicide

Death: December 3, 2002
Location: Bagram, Afghanistan
Found unresponsive, restrained in his cell
Cause: Pulmonary embolism due to blunt force injuries
to the legs
Manner of Death: Homicide

Autopsy Number: Me04-14. Date of Death: January 9th, 2004. Iraqi detainee died while in U.S. custody. This 47-year-old White male died of blunt force injuries and asphyxia. The autopsy disclosed multiple blunt force injuries, including deep contusions of the chest wall, numerous displaced rib fractures, lung contusions, and hemorrhage into the intestine. The decedent was shackled to the top of a doorframe with a gag in his mouth at the time he lost consciousness and became pulseless. The severe blunt force injuries, the hanging position, and the obstruction of the oral cavity with a gag contributed to this individual's death. The manner of death is homicide.

The ACLU filed a Freedom of Information Act request on October 7, 2003, demanding the release of information about detainees held overseas by the United States. The following e-mails, released to the ACLU along with more than 100,000 other pages describing the handling and torture of detainees, are from Federal Bureau of Investigation (FBI) personnel reporting on what they witnessed and took part in at Guantánamo. The e-mails chronicle a descent into depravity as well as the astonishment of some agents when they realize that the Department of Defense, or DOD, operates outside the rule of law.

On June 20, 2003, under the heading "Survived the first week," an FBI agent writes:

Hello! Well, I've survived my first week at GTMO. We've observed and provided observations and suggestions on 7 (or was it 8?) interviews in 6 days. Two yesterday and two the day before anyhow.... Many of the interviewers have approached us for help and in other cases we've asked if we could sit in to see new detainees, etc., and no one has said no yet. Seem to have been well received by most interviewers. Interesting differences between the interviewees, as well as interview styles. And definitely areas where I feel we've contributed. We're still hearing about folks doing weird things like subjecting interviewees to strobe lights, etc., but have not seen anything of concern to date. Overheard a very loud (non-Bureau) interview down the hall yesterday, but chose not to observe it.

And when not abusing detainees, the agents retreat into compounds for recreation. An agent reports:

On the personal front—have seen two movies at the outdoor theater (Matrix Reloaded and Bruce Almighty—definitely a must see (CENSORED), there's even a monkey scene in it for you!) There was a bonfire beach party last Fri. and a pool party on Sat. nite. We have an offer to go sailing this Sunday—not sure if going yet.

Another agent, ten days later, writes:

Following a detainee interview exact date unknown, while leaving the interview building at Camp Delta at approximately 8:30 p.m. or later, I heard and observed in the hallway loud music and flashes of light. I walked from the hallway into the open door of a monitoring room to see what was going on. From the monitoring room, I looked inside the adjacent interview room. At that time I saw another detainee sitting on the floor of the interview room with an Israeli flag draped around him, loud music being played and a strobe light flashing. I left the monitoring room immediately after seeing this activity. I

did not see any other persons inside the interview room
with the Israeli flag–draped detainee, but suspect that
this was a practice used by the DOD DHS since the only
other persons inside the hallway near this particular
interview room were dressed in green military fatigues,
similar to the ones worn by DOD DHS and the DOD MP
Uniformed Reservists. At no time did I observe any physical assaults take place of this detainee nor any others
while assigned to GTMO.

"I understood prior to deployment to GTMO, that such
techniques were not allowed," the agent added, "nor approved by FBI policy."

On May 10, 2004, an agent, writing under the heading "Instructions to GTMO Interrogators," had these
words:

> We did advise each supervisor that went to GTMO to stay
> in line with Bureau policy and not deviate from that (CEN-
> SORED). I went to GTMO with (CENSORED) early on and
> we discussed the effectiveness (CENSORED) the SSA. We
> (BAU and ITOS1) had also met with Generals Dunlevey &
> Miller explaining our position (Law Enforcement techniques)
> vs. DoD. Both agreed the Bureau has their way of doing
> business and DoD has their marching orders from the
> Sec Def. Although the two techniques differed drastically,
> both Generals believed they had a job to accomplish. It
> was our mission to gather critical intelligence and evidence
> (CENSORED) in furtherance of FBI cases. In my weekly
> meetings with DOJ we often discussed (CENSORED)
> techniques and how they were not effective or producing
> Intel that was reliable.... We all agreed (CENSORED) were
> going to be an issue in the military commission cases....
> One specific example was (CENSORED). Once the Bureau
> provide DoD with the findings (CENSORED) they wanted
> to pursue expeditiously their methods to get "more out of
> him." (CENSORED) We were given a so called deadline to use
> our traditional methods. Once our timeline (CENSORED)

was up (CENSORED) took the reigns. We stepped out of the picture and (CENSORED) ran the operation (CENSORED). FBI did not participate at the direction of myself, (CENSORED) and BAU UC (CENSORED).... Bottom line is FBI personnel have not been involved in any methods of interrogations that deviate from our policy. The specific guidance we have given has always been no Miranda, otherwise, follow FBI/DOJ policy just as you would in your field office. Use common sense. Utilize our methods that are proven.

On October 26, 2002, in a subject heading titled "GTMO Update," an agent writes this:

Hello all, (CENSORED) is gone and I am here. (CENSORED) you made quite an impression and have left big shoes to fill. First impressions: It is hot here. I brought too much luggage. The learning curve is vertical. The more you read about Islam and our friends here the better off you will be once you get here. Many different agendas here and you will have to use all of your behavioral skills to pull it all together and keep your finger on the pulse ... no one will lead you by the hand. Did I mention that it is hot here? ... Later.

On July 12, 2004, there is this e-mail:

Mr. (CENSORED), I am responding to your request for feedback on aggressive treatment and improper interview techniques used on detainees at GTMO. I did observe treatment that was not only aggressive, but personally very upsetting, although I can't say that this treatment was perpetrated by Bureau employees. It seemed that these techniques were being employed by the military, government contract employees, and (CENSORED).

And in a December 5, 2003, message with the subject heading "Impersonating FBI at GTMO" is this note:

I am forwarding this EC up the CTD chain of command. MLDU requested this information be documented to protect the FBI. MLDU has had a long standing and documented position against the use of some of DOD's interrogation practices, however, we were not aware of these latest techniques until recently.

Of concern, DOD interrogators impersonating Supervisory Special Agents of the FBI told a detainee that (CENSORED). These same interrogation teams then (CENSORED). The detainee was also told by this interrogation team (CENSORED).

These tactics have produced no intelligence of a threat neutralization nature to date and CITF believes that techniques have destroyed any chance of prosecuting this detainee.

If this detainee is released or his story made public in any way, DOD interrogators will not be held accountable because these torture techniques were done by the "FBI" interrogators. The FBI will be left holding the bag before the public.

Henry Giroux's *Hearts of Darkness* makes a compelling case that these stories are not stories of the other. They are the stories of us. Torture begins as a tool promoted to protect us and ends with our physical subjugation. Torture eradicates the rule of law. It maims and kills all who come within its orbit. As Giroux makes clear, no one is exempt, not even children. We can halt torture now, or we can become its victim. These are the only choices.

—Chris Hedges
Senior Fellow at The Nation Institute

◊

Preface and Acknowledgments

Since the turn of the twenty-first century, we have lived through an historical period in which the United States relinquished its tenuous claim to democracy. The frames through which democracy apprehends others as human beings worthy of respect, dignity, and human rights were sacrificed to a mode of politics and culture that simply became an extension of war, both at home and abroad. At home, the punishing state increasingly replaced the welfare state, however ill conceived, as more and more individuals and groups were treated as disposable populations, undeserving of those safety nets and basic protections that provide the conditions for living with a sense of security and dignity. Under such conditions, basic social supports were replaced by an accelerated production of prisons, the expansion of the criminal justice system into everyday life, and the further erosion of crucial civil liberties. Shared responsibilities gave way to shared fears, and the only distinction that seemed to resonate in the culture was between friends and patriots on one hand and dissenters and enemies on the other. State violence not only became acceptable, it was normalized as the government spied on its citizens, suspended the right of habeas corpus, sanctioned police brutality against those who questioned state power, relied on the state secrets privilege to hide its crimes, and increasingly reduced public spheres designed to protect children to containment centers and warehouses that modeled themselves after prisons. Fear both altered the landscape of democratic rights and values and dehumanized a population that was ever more willing to look the other way as large segments of the populace were either dehumanized, incarcerated, or simply treated as disposable. The dire consequences can be seen every day as the media report a stream of tragic stories about decent people losing their homes; more and more young people being incarcerated; and growing numbers of people living in their cars, on the streets, or in tent cities. The *New York Times* offers up a front-page story about young people leaving their recession-ridden families in order to live on the street, often surviving by selling their bodies for money. Reports surface in the dominant media about unspeakable horrors being inflicted on children tortured in the "death chambers" of Iraq, Cuba, and Afghanistan. And the American people barely blink.

The Bush administration further eroded a culture inspired by democratic values, replacing it with a culture of war and a culture of illegality that experimented with an extrajudicial detention system used to create torture chambers in Bagram, Kandahar, and Guantánamo Bay. After 2001, the language and ghostly shadow of war became all-embracing, not only blurring the distinction between war and peace but also putting into play a public pedagogy in which every aspect of the culture was shaped by militarized knowledge, values, and ideals. From video games and Hollywood films either supported or produced by the Department of Defense to the ongoing militarization of public and higher education, the notion of the common good was subordinated to a military metaphysics, warlike values, and the dictates of the national security state. War gained a new status under the Bush administration, moving from an option of last resort to a primary instrument of diplomacy in the war on terror. A dogmatic faith in war was supplemented by a persistent attempt to legitimate such a politics through another kind of war based on pedagogical struggle to create subjects, citizens, and institutions that would support such draconian policies. War was no longer the last resort of a state intent on defending its territory; it morphed into a new form of public pedagogy—a type of cultural war machine—designed to shape and lead the society. War became the foundation for a politics that employed military language, concepts, and policing relations to address problems far beyond the familiar terrains of battle. In some cases, war was so aestheticized by the dominant media that it resembled an advertisement for a tourist industry. The upshot is that the meaning of war was rhetorically, visually, and materially expanded to name, legitimate, and wage battles against social problems involving drugs, poverty, and the nation's newfound enemy, the Mexican immigrant.

As war became normalized as the central function of power and politics, it became a regular and normative element of American society, legitimated by a state of exception and emergency that became permanent rather than temporary. As the production of violence reached beyond traditionally defined enemies and threats, the state now took aim at terrorism, shifting its register of power by waging war on a concept, broadening its pursuits, tactics, and strategies against no specific state, army, soldiers, or location. The enemy was omnipresent, all the more difficult to root out and all the more convenient for expanding the tactics of surveillance, the culture of fear, and the resources of violence. War was now a permanent and commonplace feature of American domestic and foreign policy, a battle that had no definitive end and demanded the constant use of violence. War had become more than a military strategy: it was now a pedagogy and a form of cultural politics designed to legitimate certain modes of governance, create identities supportive of militaristic values, and provide the formative culture that supported the organization and production of violence as a central feature of domestic and foreign policy.

It is difficult to imagine how any democracy can avoid being corrupted when war becomes the foundation of politics, if not culture itself. Any democracy that makes war and state violence the organizing principles of society cannot survive for long, at least as a democratic entity. The United States descended into a period in which society was increasingly organized through the production of both symbolic and material violence. A culture of cruelty emerged in the media, especially in the talk radio circuit, in which a sordid nationalism combined with a hypermilitarism and masculinity that scorned not merely reason but also all those who fit into the stereotype of other—which appeared to include everyone who was not white and Christian. Dialogue, reason, and thoughtfulness slowly disappeared from the public realm as every encounter was framed within circles of certainty, staged as a fight to the death. As the civic and moral center of the country disappeared under the Bush administration, the language of the marketplace provided the only referent for understanding the obligations of citizenship and global responsibility, undeterred by a growing war machine and culture that produced jobs and goods and furthered the war economy.

The war abroad entered a new phase with the release of the photos of detainees being tortured at Abu Ghraib prison. War as organized violence was stripped of its noble aims and delusional goal of promoting democracy, revealing state violence at its most degrading and dehumanizing moment. State power had become an instrument of torture, ripping into the flesh of human beings, raping women, and most abominably torturing children. Democracy had become something that defended the unthinkable and inflicted the most horrible mutilations on both adults and children deemed to be the enemies of democracy. But the mutilations were also inflicted against the body politic as politicians such as former vice president Dick Cheney defended torture while the media addressed the question of torture not as a violation of democratic principles or human rights but as a strategy that might or might not produce concrete information. The utilitarian arguments used to defend a market-driven economy that only recognized cost-benefit analyses and the priority of exchange values had now reached their logical end point as similar arguments were used to defend torture, even when it involved children. The pretense of democracy was stripped bare as it was revealed over and over again that the United States had become a torture state, aligning itself with infamous dictatorships such as those in Argentina and Chile during the 1970s. The U.S. government under the Bush administration had finally arrived at a point where the metaphysics of war, organized violence, and state terrorism prevented leaders in Washington from recognizing how much they were emulating the very acts of terrorism they claimed to be fighting.

The circle had now been completed, as the warfare state had been transformed into a torture state. Everything became permissible both at home and abroad, just as the legal system along with the market system legitimated a punishing and ruthless mode of economic Darwinism that viewed morality, if not democracy itself, as a weakness to be either scorned or ignored. Markets not only drove politics, they also removed ethical considerations from any understanding of how markets worked or what effects they produced on the larger social order. Self-regulation trumped moral considerations and became the primary force driving the market, while narrowly defined individual interests set the parameters of what was possible. The public collapsed into the private, and social responsibility was reduced to the arbitrary desires of the hermetic, asocial self. Not surprisingly, the inhuman and degrading entered public discourse and shaped the debate about war, state violence, and human rights abuses; it also served to legitimate such practices. The United States unabashedly entered into a moral vacuum that enabled it to both justify torture and state violence and to mobilize successfully a war culture and public pedagogy in the larger culture that convinced, as a Pew Research Center poll indicated, 54 percent of the American people that "torture is at least sometimes justified to gain important information from suspected terrorists."[1] Torture was normalized and duly accepted by the majority of the American people while the promise of an aspiring democracy was irreparably damaged.

Hearts of Darkness: Torturing Children in the War on Terror examines how the United States under the Bush administration embarked on a war on terror that not only defended torture as a matter of official policy but also furthered the conditions for the emergence of a culture of cruelty that profoundly altered the political and moral landscape of the country. As torture became normalized under Bush, it corrupted American ideals and political culture, and the administration passed over to the dark side in sanctioning the unimaginable and unspeakable—the torture of children. Although the rise of the torture state has been a subject of intense controversy, too little has been said by intellectuals, academics, artists, writers, parents, and politicians about how state violence under the Bush administration set in motion a public pedagogy and political culture that legitimated the systemic torture of children and did so with the complicity of dominant media that either denied such practices or simply ignored them. The focus on children here is deliberate because young people provide a powerful referent for the long-term consequences of social policies, if not the future itself, and also because they offer a crucial index to measure the moral and democratic values of a nation. Children are the heartbeat and moral compass of politics because they speak to the best of its possibilities and promises, and yet they have, since the 1980s, become the vanishing point of moral debate, either deemed irrelevant because of their age, discounted because they are largely viewed as commodities, or scorned because they are considered a threat to adult society. I have written elsewhere that how a society educates its youth is connected to the collective future the people hope for. Actually, how youth were educated became meaningless as a moral issue under the Bush administration because youth were not only devalued and considered unworthy of a decent life and future (one reason they were denied adequate health care), they were also reduced to the status of the inhuman and depraved and were subjected to cruel acts of torture in sites that were as illegal as they were barbaric. In this instance, youth became the negation of politics and of the future itself.

But more is at stake here than making such crimes visible: there is also the moral and political imperative of raising serious questions about the challenges the Obama administration must address in light of this shameful period in American history, especially if it wants to reverse such policies and make a claim on restoring any vestige of American democracy. Of course, when a country makes torture legal and extends the disciplinary mechanisms of pain, humiliation, and suffering to children, it suggests that far too many people looked away while this was happening and in doing so allowed conditions to emerge that made the unspeakable act of justifying the torture of children a matter of state policy. It is time for Americans to face up to these crimes and engage in a national dialogue about the political, economic, educational, and social conditions that allowed such a dark period to emerge in American history and to hold accountable those who were responsible for such acts. The Obama administration is under fire for its embrace of many of Bush's policies, but what is most disturbing is its willingness to make war, secrecy, and the suspension of civil liberties central features of its own policies. In his desire to look ahead and embrace a depoliticizing and morally empty notion of postpartisan politics, Obama recycles a dangerous form of historical and social amnesia, while overlooking the political and civic pathology he inherited. Hopefully, this book will remind us that memory at its best is unsettling and sometimes even dangerous in its call for individuals to become moral and political witnesses; to take risks; and to embrace history not merely as a critique but also as a warning about how fragile democracy is and what will often happen when the principles, ideals, and elements of the culture that sustain it are allowed to slip away, overtaken by forces that embrace death rather than life, fear rather than hope, insularity rather than solidarity. Robert Hass, the American poet, has suggested that the job of education, its political job, "is to refresh the idea of justice going dead in us all the time."[2] Justice is slipping away, once again, under the Obama administration, but it is not just the government's job to keep it from "going dead": it is also the job of all Americans—as parents, citizens, individuals, and educators—not merely as a matter of social obligation or moral responsibility but also as an act of politics, agency, and possibility.

This book is divided into six chapters. The first chapter analyzes the emergence of a set of predatory economic, social, and political conditions that were intensified, particularly under the administration of George W. Bush, setting the stage for the transformation of the welfare state into the warfare and torture state. As democratic values were increasingly subordinated to market values and as a culture of fear replaced a culture of compassion, restraints previously placed on the play of market and financial forces were removed. Public issues now collapsed into private concerns, and people became more vulnerable to those economic and political forces promoting uncertainty, instability, and insecurity. As any notion of the common good and the institutions that supported it were increasingly viewed with disdain, the culture became more self-absorbed, mean-spirited, competitive, and ruthless in its unwillingness to show compassion for the other, especially those who were most vulnerable to uncertain times—the young, the elderly, the immigrants, the poor minorities, and the Muslims.

As the culture of fear and competitiveness seemed to spin out of control, the punishing state replaced the social state, and politics was largely reduced to protecting the benefits of the rich and expanding those policing apparatuses that were used to contain and punish the poor. As more and more social problems were criminalized, the punishing state became the sole source of legitimation for a state weakened by the forces of a destructive globalization and the free-floating forces of capital and finance. As the laws of the market, an excessive individualism, and an unchecked notion of self-interest became the most important principles shaping society, democratic values, identities, and relations were subordinated to the interests of an economic formation that had freed itself from all constraints. The conditions were now developing in which matters of justice, human rights, and truth were sacrificed to the forces of political and economic expediency. In the second chapter of the book, I analyze how torture became state policy through a series of "illegal legalities" concocted by various members of the Bush administration and how the media, in collusion with the government, refused to acknowledge that torture was not something that simply emerged in the aftermath of 9/11 but had been practiced by the U.S. government for decades. In the third chapter, I analyze how the debate about torture seemed to free itself from human rights abuses committed by the United States historically and how the Bush administration actively promoted new forms of torture in violation of every major international treaty dealing with torture as an illegal and criminal act. The fourth chapter details the government denial of state-legitimated torture and the gruesome acts of violence and abuse committed on numerous detainees in various U.S.-controlled sites and prisons. Chapter 5 provides ample evidence of how these various conditions along with numerous violations of human rights ultimately resulted in the unthinkable—the torture of children. This chapter is as detailed as it is shocking, invoking both testimony from third parties and testimony from children who were actually tortured. The final chapter of the book raises a series of questions about whether Obama will challenge the horrible legacy of the Bush administration by redefining American democracy or whether he will simply become another victim of the culture of cruelty and suffering that is the legacy of the Bush-Cheney years.

I want to thank, once again, Susan Searls Giroux for her critical reading of this manuscript. Needless to say, it is much better because of her keen eye and critical insights. She was writing her own book on race and the university while taking the time to read this work. My life would be so incomplete without her love and support. My colleague Grace Pollock has been invaluable in editing this book. Every time she intervenes in my work, she creates something akin to poetry. I am truly grateful for her insights and rigorous interventions. Maya Sabados, my longtime administrative assistant, tirelessly read a number of drafts, always offering new insights and catching my endless typos. I am also grateful to Victoria Harper, who published in *Truthout* a small excerpt from the book. She has been a critical supporter of my work and has helped me develop a public voice, for which I am deeply appreciative. My colleague and friend David Clark provided remarkably brilliant insights into how to shape this work. I would also like to thank Ken Saltman, Christopher Robbins, Olivia Ward, Cary Fraser, Ira Shor, Sophia McClennen, Tolu Olorunda, and Doug Morris, who have all been both supportive and helpful with their readings of the text. Although my two canine companions, Miles and Kaya, never read the manuscript, they provided the kind of invaluable support that only animal lovers could understand.

◆

Chapter One

The War on Terror and the Culture of Cruelty

"How does one man assert his power over another,
Winston?"

Winston thought. "By making him suffer," he said.

"Exactly. By making him suffer. Obedience is not
enough."

—*George Orwell, 1984*[1]

By almost any political, economic, or ethical measure,
Barack Obama inherited, with his election victory in 2008,
a set of problems produced by one of the darkest periods
in American history.[2] In the eight years prior to Obama's
presidency, the spaces, however weakly constituted, where
genuine politics could occur largely disappeared as a result
of both the suppression of dissent and an ongoing assault
by the market-driven forces of privatization, deregulation,
and unrestrained greed. Beyond that, there was a radical hardening of the culture that increasingly disparaged
democratic values, human dignity, and the safety nets
provided by the state. George W. Bush, the privileged and
profligate son of a wealthy Texas oilman, became the em-
bodiment of a political culture in which willful immaturity
and stubborn civic illiteracy found its match in an emerging

1

culture of excess and irresponsibility.[3] As finance capital reigned supreme over American society, democratization, along with the public spheres needed to sustain it, became an unsettled and increasingly fragile, perhaps even dysfunctional project. As the social state was dismantled, the hypermasculine, competitive, and predatory values of the neoliberal market—now mediated through reality TV and popular culture in general—became the organizing principles of a society in which both the tools of democracy and the egalitarian and humanistic values they support were viewed with contempt or simply ignored. The issue of bearing responsibility for others gave way to a cultural politics endlessly marketed through a variety of entertainment sites. Zygmunt Bauman, the renowned sociologist, sums it up perfectly: "They all tell us the same story: that one is of use to other human beings only as long as she or he can be exploited to their advantage, that the waste bin, the ultimate destination of the excluded, is the natural prospect for those who no longer fit or no longer wish to be exploited in such a way, that survival is the name of the game of human togetherness and that the ultimate stake of survival is outliving the others."[4] The standard for politics now seemed to be achieving escape from any sense of moral, political, and social responsibility—most egregiously manifested in the rise of a society that was willing to torture not only those considered enemies of the state but also children caught up in Bush's war on terrorism.[5]

Democratic values were increasingly and insistently subordinated to market values, and the obligations of citizenship were emptied of any meaning and viewed largely through the lens of consumerism.[6] The continual privatization and deregulation of society were matched by the ongoing depoliticization of the public sphere, in which the only questions worth asking were those dictated by market-driven forces. The shared conditions on which human life depended dwindled as public spheres became commercialized and privatized, even as shared responsibilities gave way to individual fears buttressed by the stark demands of competitiveness, efficiency, and the recasting of citizens as isolated consumers.[7] Public concerns collapsed into private issues, and it became more difficult to connect individual problems with social problems. With the bonds of sociality dismembered, stunned and isolated individuals negotiated life's problems as best they could—like so many amputees willfully forgetting or fitfully haunted by phantom limbs.[8] Pressing social issues, such as the growing ecological crisis, skyrocketing levels of unemployment, wage stagnation, homelessness, poverty, and an unprecedented war debt, lost their political capacity to compel citizens to organize and act. Privatized utopias of neoliberal consumerist society offered the public only a market-based language that produced narrow modes of subjectivity, defining what people should know and how they should act within the constricted interests and values of what Bauman has called "an order of egoism."[9] As market forces and a growing authoritarianism produced new modes of social de-skilling, Americans were prompted to deride, if not view as personal weakness, any sense of social responsibility toward others; at the same time, they were refusing to assume any civic responsibility for challenging the accelerating assault by the Bush administration on democratic public spheres, institutions, policies, and social relations. As democracy became more dysfunctional, an ever-expanding culture of cruelty and punishment emerged, in which immigrants, the homeless, poor minorities of color, a reserve army of the permanently unemployed, and children—even and especially poor children of color—were portrayed disparagingly and increasingly viewed as expendable in the mainstream media and on right-wing talk radio.

As an analogue to the superfluity of the new Gilded Age, the tawdry excesses of the rich and powerful were celebrated—at once objects of public and political envy and veneration.[10] Finance capital intensified the trend toward depressed wages and was augmented by a credit binge fueled by desperate attempts on the part of individuals and working families to stay afloat in an economy of spiraling debt and widespread insecurity and instability. A nation of consumers soon gave way to a nation of debtors, many of whom increasingly became part of a large army of unemployed, homeless, and destitute citizens. As much feared as condemned, a plague of failed consumers emerged only to disappear silently into the ranks of the chronically unemployed or be forcefully inducted into a criminal justice system that qualifies the United States as the largest jailer in the world—incarcerating nearly 3 million people in an apartheid-based prison system. With democracy in retreat in a post–9/11 world saturated by a culture of fear and uncertainty, public life was more and more militarized, shredding all vestiges of civil liberties, civic agency, and compassion for those who deviated from normative expectations by religion, race, class, age, and ethnicity; meanwhile, dissent was increasingly treated as un-American. Under the Bush administration, a seeping, sometimes galloping authoritarianism began to reach into every corner of the culture, giving free reign to those antidemocratic forces in which religious, market, military, and political fundamentalism thrived, casting an ominous shadow over the fate of U.S. democracy.

Public spaces, which once kept hope alive by creating the conditions for debate, informed dialogue, reflexive thoughtfulness, and civic engagement, were further commercialized, subject to surveillance, treated with cynical disdain by both politicians and the media, and increasingly committed to political theater, or they simply "disappeared" altogether. Politics was reduced to a spectacle, a type of tabloid shock and awe to mesmerize the populace and largely organized around celebrity gossip and the trade in personal insult, punctuated now and again by revelations about a scandal (often sexual, occasionally political) that gave newsworthiness to the life of an elected official.[11] Consequently, as argued by the writers of *Left Turn*, "electability [has been] equated by the media almost exclusively with how well the campaign can raise enough money to invest in the institutions of the spectacle."[12] The tragic legacy of this recent period in American politics is perhaps most visible in the rise of an imperial presidency; an unjustified war in Iraq; an assault on the human rights of Arabs and Muslims; an erosion of civil liberties; a reenergized misogyny; the growing incarceration of people of color; and a militant attack on workers, unions, and the poor. It is also evident in a most shocking and brutal abdication of adults' duty to care for and protect children who are not their own. Flash points—such as Hurricane Katrina and Hurricane Rita, Abu Ghraib prison, the Enron scandal, the subprime mortgage crisis, the Bernie Madoff debacle, preventive detention, warrantless wiretapping, "black sites," and Guantánamo—dramatically illustrated both the growing crisis of democratic values and a cartography of power that indicated an emerging dark side of political culture.

Under the Bush administration, power became an instrument of retribution and punishment connected to and fueled by a repressive state. A bullying rhetoric of war, a ruthless consolidation of economic forces, an all-embracing neoliberal market apparatus, and a media-driven pedagogy of fear supported and sustained a distinct culture of cruelty and inequality in the United States. In pointing to a culture of cruelty, I am not employing a form of leftist moralism that collapses matters of power and politics into the discourse of character. On the contrary, I think the notion of a culture of cruelty is useful in thinking through the convergence of everyday life and politics, in considering material relations of power—the disciplining of the body as an object of control—on the one hand, and the production of cultural meaning, especially the co-optation of popular culture to sanction official violence, on the other. The culture of cruelty signals how politics is inscribed in dominant relations of power and suggests how life and death now converge so as to fundamentally transform the way in which we think about and imagine politics in the current historical moment.

A growing number of individuals and groups now find themselves living in a society that measures the worth of human life in terms of cost-benefit analyses. The central issue of life and politics is no longer about working to get ahead but struggling simply to survive.[13] And many groups who are considered marginal because they are poor, unemployed, of color, elderly, or young have not just been excluded from "the American dream" but also have become utterly redundant and disposable, waste products of a society that no longer considers them of any value.[14] How else can we explain the zealousness with which social safety nets have been dismantled, the transition from welfare to workfare (offering few job-training programs and no child care), and recent acrimony over health care reform's public option? What accounts for the ratification of laws that criminalize the behavior of the 1.2 million homeless in the United States, often defining sleeping, sitting, soliciting, lying down, or loitering in a public place as a criminal offense rather than a behavior in need of compassionate goodwill and public assistance? Or, for that matter, how can we account for the expulsions, suspensions, segregation, class discrimination, and racism in the public schools as well as the more severe beatings, broken bones, and damaged lives endured by young people in the juvenile justice system? Within this politics, largely stoked by a market fundamentalism that both "registers a shift in the generic nature of power"[15] and only values wealth, money, and consumers, there is a ruthless and hidden dimension of cruelty, one in which the powers of life and death are more and more determined by disciplinary apparatuses (such as the criminal justice system for many poor people of color) and/or a market sovereignty that increasingly decides "who may live and who may die."[16] The growing dominance of right-wing media forged in a pedagogy of hate has become a crucial element, providing numerous platforms for a culture of cruelty, and it is fundamental to how we understand the role of public pedagogy in a range of sites outside traditional forms of schooling. This educational apparatus and mode of public pedagogy are central to analyzing how "power is exercised, reinforced, and contested"[17] in a growing culture of cruelty. This public pedagogy of hate must be acknowledged because it plays a formative role in how particular identities, desires, and needs are mobilized in support of an overt racism, hostility toward immigrants, and utter disdain coupled with the threat of mob violence directed at any political figure supportive of the social contract and the welfare state. Citizens are increasingly constructed through a language of contempt for all noncommercial public spheres and a chilling indifference to the plight of others that is more and more often expressed in vicious tirades against big government and health care reform. There is a growing element of scorn on the part of the American public for those human beings caught in the web of misfortune, human suffering, dependency, and deprivation. As the progressive writer Barbara Ehrenreich observes,

> The pattern is to curtail financing for services that might help the poor while ramping up law enforcement: starve school and public transportation budgets, then make truancy illegal. Shut down public housing, then make it a crime to be homeless. Be sure to harass street vendors when there are few other opportunities for employment. The experience of the poor, and especially poor minorities, comes to resemble that of a rat in a cage scrambling to avoid erratically administered electric shocks.[18]

A right-wing spin machine, influenced by haters such as Rush Limbaugh, Glenn Beck, Michael Savage, and Ann Coulter, endlessly spews out a toxic rhetoric in which, for example, all Muslims are defined as jihadists; the homeless are not victims of misfortune but are just lazy; blacks are not terrorized by a racist criminal justice system but are the main architects of a culture of criminality; the epidemic of obesity has nothing to do with corporations, big agriculture, and advertisers selling junk food but is rather the result of "big" government giving people food stamps; and the public sphere is largely for white people, who are being threatened by immigrants and people of color. Glenn Beck, the alleged voice of the common man, appearing on the *Fox & Friends* morning show, calls President Obama a "racist" and then accuses him of "having a deep-seated hatred for white people or the white culture."[19] Nationally syndicated radio host Rush Limbaugh once unapologetically mused on the air: "Have you ever noticed how all composite pictures of wanted criminals resemble Jesse Jackson?"[20] His counterpart in right-wing hate, talk radio host Michael Savage, states on his show: "You know, when I see a woman walking around with a burqa, I see a Nazi. That's what I see—how do you like that?—a hateful Nazi who would like to cut your throat and kill your children."[21] He also claims that Obama is "surrounded by terrorists" and is "raping America." This appears to be a variation of a crude theme established by Ann Coulter, who refers to Bill Clinton as a "very good rapist."[22] Even worse, Obama is described as a "neo-Marxist fascist dictator in the making" who plans to "force children into a paramilitary domestic army."[23] And this is just a small sampling of the kind of hate talk that permeates right-wing media. This hostile rhetoric could be dismissed as loony right-wing political theater if it were not for the low levels of civic literacy displayed by the many Americans who choose to believe and invest in this type of hate talk.[24] Though it may be idiocy, it reveals a powerful set of political, economic, and educational forces at work in miseducating the American public, while at the same time extending the culture of cruelty. One central task of any viable form of democratic politics is to analyze the culture of cruelty and its overt and covert dimensions of violence, which often parade as entertainment. This task is particularly useful for rethinking and reformulating how specific mechanisms of politics, corporate influence, and public pedagogy work to make power invisible, while also exercising a ruthless mode of sovereignty that, as critical theorist Judith Butler argues, both legitimates and creates the conditions in which some lives are not recognized as human or "grievable" and are thus subject to unimaginable forms of pain and violence.[25]

Underlying the culture of cruelty that reached its apogee during the Bush administration was the legalization of state violence, such that human suffering was now sanctioned by the law, which no longer served as a summons to justice. And as a legal culture emerged that made violence and human suffering socially acceptable, popular culture rendered such violence pleasurable by commodifying, aestheticizing, and spectacularizing it. Rather than being unspoken and unseen, violence in American life has become both visible in its pervasiveness and normalized as a central feature of dominant and popular culture. Americans have grown accustomed to luxuriating in a warm bath of cinematic blood, as young people and adults alike are seduced with commercial and military video games such as *Grand Theft Auto* and *America's Army*;[26] the television series *24* and its ongoing bacchanalian fete of torture; the crude violence on display in World Wrestling Entertainment and Ultimate Fighting Championship; and an endless series of vigilante films such as *The Brave One* (2007) and *Law Abiding Citizen* (2009), in which the rule of law is suspended by the viscerally satisfying images of men and women seeking revenge as laudable killing machines—a nod to the permanent state of emergency and war in the United States. Symptomatically, there is the mindless glorification and aestheticization of brutal violence in the most celebrated Hollywood films, including many of Quentin Tarantino's films, especially *Kill Bill 1* and *Kill Bill 2* (2003, 2004), *Death Proof* (2007), and *Inglourious Basterds* (2009). In the case of the most recent Tarantino release, in fact, the press reported that Dianne Kruger, the costar of the bloody war film *Inglourious Basterds*, claimed she "loved being tortured by Brad Pitt [though] she was frustrated she didn't get an opportunity to get frisky with her co-star, but admits being beaten by Pitt was a satisfying experience."[27] This is more than the aestheticization of violence; it is the normalization and glorification of torture itself.

If Hollywood has made gratuitous violence the main staple of its endless parade of blockbuster films, then television has tapped into the culture of cruelty in a way that was unimaginable before the attack on the United States on September 11, 2001. Prime-time television before the attacks had "fewer than four acts of torture" per year, but "now there are more than a hundred."[28] Moreover, the people who torture are no longer the villains but instead are the heroes of prime-time television. The most celebrated is, of course, Jack Bauer, the tragic-ethical hero of the wildly popular Fox TV thriller *24*. Torture is the main thread running through the show's plots, often presented "with gusto and no moral compunction,"[29] while Bauer is portrayed as a patriot, rather than a depraved monster, who tortures in order to protect American lives and national security. Torture in this scenario takes society's ultimate betrayal of human dignity and legitimates the pain and fear it produces as acceptable, all the while turning a "moral sadist" into a television celebrity.[30] The show has over 15 million viewers, and its glamorization of torture has proven so successful that it appears to have not only numbed the public's reaction to the horrors of torture but has also influenced the U.S. military to such a degree that the Pentagon sent Brig. Gen. Patrick Finnegan to California to meet with the producers of the show. "He told them that promoting illegal behavior in the series ... was having a damaging effect on young troops."[31]

The glorification of gratuitous, sadistic violence is also on full display in the popular HBO television series *Dexter*, which portrays a serial killer as a sympathetic, even lovable, character. With the advent of the Internet and a seemingly endless public appetite for more violent forms of pornography, the merging of sex, violence, and sadism has become mainstream and a lucrative source of profits for the entertainment industry. But the discourse of violence, sadism, and torture does more than reconstitute what counts as the new, more brutalizing face of screen culture; it also, as Pulitzer Prize–winning journalist and veteran war correspondent Chris Hedges points out, reflects the pathology of a new kind of pornography and

> the endemic cruelty of our society.... Porn reflects back the cruelty of a culture that tosses its mentally ill out on the street, warehouses more than 2 million people in prisons, denies health care to tens of millions of the poor, champions gun ownership over gun control, and trumpets an obnoxious and superpatriotic nationalism and rapacious corporate capitalism. The violence, cruelty and degradation of porn are expressions of a society that has lost the capacity for empathy.[32]

What these examples make clear is that visual spectacles steeped in degradation and violence now permeate the culture and garner popularity and critical acclaim far beyond anything found previously in reality TV shows, professional wrestling, and the infamous *Jerry Springer Show*. These earlier programs, though appealing to more narrow audiences, also traded in fantasy, glamorized violence, and escapism. As Hedges discusses in his analysis of professional wrestling, this more recent cultural fare mirrors the worst dimensions of an unchecked and unregulated market society in which "winning is all that matters. Morality is irrelevant.... It is all about personal pain, vendettas, hedonism, and fantasies of revenge, while inflicting pain on others. It is the cult of victimhood."[33] The celebration of hyperviolence, moral sadism, and torture has traveled easily from fiction to real life since 2005 with the emergence of a proliferation of "bum fight" videos on the Internet, "shot by young men and boys who are seen beating the homeless or who pay transients a few dollars to fight each other."[34] The culture of cruelty mimics cinematic violence as the agents of abuse both indulge in actual forms of violence and then celebrate the barbarity by posting it on the Web, betraying a narcissistic desire for fame and recognition while voyeuristically consuming their own violent cultural productions. The National Coalition for the Homeless claims that "on YouTube in July 2009, people have posted 85,900 videos with 'bum' in the title [and] 5,690 videos can be found with the title 'bum fight,' representing ... an increase of 1,460 videos since April 2008."[35] Rather than problematize violence, popular culture increasingly normalizes it, often in ways that border on criminal intent. For instance, a recent issue of *Maxim*, a popular men's magazine, included "a blurb titled 'Hunt the Homeless' [focusing on] a coming 'hobo convention' in Iowa and says 'Kill one for fun. We're 87 percent sure it's legal.'"[36] In this context, violence is not simply being transformed into an utterly distasteful form of adolescent entertainment or spectacularized to attract readers and boost profits— it becomes a powerful pedagogical force in the culture of cruelty by aligning itself with the very real surge of violence against the homeless, often committed by young men and teenage boys looking for a thrill.[37] Spurred on by the always reassuring presence of violence and dehumanization in the wider culture, these young "thrill offenders" now search out the homeless and "punch, kick, shoot or set afire people living on the streets, frequently killing them, simply for the sport of it, their victims all but invisible to society."[38] All these elements of popular culture speak stylishly and sadistically to new ways in which to maximize the pleasure of violence, giving it a hip (and fascist) edginess.

Needless to say, neither violent video games and television series nor Hollywood films and the Internet (or, for that matter, popular culture in general) cause in any direct sense real-world violence and suffering, but they do not leave the real world behind either. That is too simplistic. What they do achieve is the execution of a well-funded and highly seductive public pedagogical enterprise that sexualizes and stylizes representations of violence, investing them with an intense pleasure quotient. I do not believe it is an exaggeration to claim that the violence of screen culture entertains and cleanses young people of the burden of ethical considerations when they, for instance, play video games that enable them to "casually kill the simulated human beings whose world they control."[39] Hollywood films such as the *Saw* series offer up a form of torture porn in which the spectacle of the violence both enhances the movies' attractiveness and offers young viewers a space where questions of ethics and responsibility are gleefully suspended, enabling them to evade their complicity in a culture of cruelty. No warnings appear on the labels of these violent videos and films, suggesting that the line between catharsis and desensitization may become blurred and making it more difficult to raise questions about what it means "to live in a society that produces, markets, and supports such products."[40] But these hyperviolent cultural products also form part of a corrupt pedagogical assemblage that obscures the hard realities of power and material violence at work through militarism, a winner-take-all economy marked by punishing inequalities, and a national security state that exhibits an utter disregard for human suffering—even the suffering of children, we must note, as when government officials refer to the lives of babies and young children lost in Iraq and Afghanistan as "collateral damage." Tragically, the crime here is much more than symbolic. Thomas Hilde has rightly insisted that "if cruelty is the worst thing that humans do to each other, torture [is] the most extreme expression of human cruelty."[41] In the immediate aftermath of the horrific events of September 11, 2001, the Bush administration began to put into place a set of laws, policies, and clandestine practices that provided the foundation for a state-sponsored culture of cruelty. Hints of such a culture were first introduced by Vice President Dick Cheney when he appeared on *Meet the Press* on September 16, 2001. Commenting on how the administration was going to respond to the attack, he uttered what has become a most memorable, if chilling, statement:

> We'll have to work sort of the dark side, if you will. We've got to spend time in the shadows in the intelligence. A lot of what needs to be done here will have to be done quietly, without any discussion, using sources and methods that are available to our intelligence agencies—if we are going to be successful. That's the world these folks operate in. And, uh, so it's going to be vital for us to use any means at our disposal basically, to achieve our objectives.[42]

Cheney's statement signaled both an attempt to expand governmental power in the war on terror and a concerted effort to put into play a vast (il)legal and repressive apparatus that expanded the field of violence and the technologies, legalities, knowledges, and institutions central to fighting such a war. Government lawyers were now enlisted to provide legal justification for acts formerly considered illegal. Insisting that President Bush had practically unlimited war powers, the Office of Legal Council (OLC) of the U.S. Department of Justice produced a series of memos and reports that sought to distinguish torture from interrogation so as to basically redefine it right out of existence.

Hilde summarizes an OLC report written in August 2002: "Torture could only be considered such when pain brought death, organ failure, serious impairment of body functions, or post-traumatic stress disorder. Moreover, the OLC Report continued, torture law does not apply to interrogations ordered by the U.S. President in the use of his powers in the war on terror. And anyway, the Report concluded, self-defense or necessity justify torture."[43] The bar for defining torture was now raised so high that it could deflect almost any existing legal definition of the term, rendering internationally agreed-on prohibitions against torture almost meaningless. Under the Bush administration, torture was renamed as "enhanced interrogation" and redefined so as to make the pain of others—including children—invisible and unaccountable, enabling its categorical denial.[44] As conservative commentator Andrew Sullivan argues, the clarity of language needed to be obscured by a form of "professionalism and bureaucratic mastery that chills in the end. . . . As Orwell predicted, the English language had to disappear first. The president referred to waterboarding prisoners as 'asking them questions.' Bringing prisoners' temperatures down to hypothermia levels was simply an 'alternative set of procedures.' And the full range of abusive practices is about 'enhanced interrogation.'"[45] As critical theorist Tzvetan Todorov notes, the Bush administration's reasoning on torture "proceeds from a form of magical thinking insofar as it pretends that [it] can act on things by changing their name."[46] According to this logic, the reality of torture and the systematic pain and suffering it causes will suddenly disappear because it has been given a new name. Needless to say, "it is not because we say that the systematic destruction of a person will not be called torture that it ceases to be torture."[47]

Under the Bush administration, as Professor Elaine Scarry has written in another context, torture translates "all of the objectified elements of pain into the insignia of power, the conversion of the enlarged map of human suffering into an emblem of the regime's strength."[48] Torture now becomes an element of power that is built on a "willed amorality."[49] Barbaric acts such as waterboarding—which had been prohibited by a number of international laws, including the Geneva Conventions, the Universal Declaration of Human Rights, and the International Covenant on Civil and Political Rights—were eagerly embraced by the Bush administration as valuable tools in the permanent war on terror. Torture acquired legal cover, providing those who engaged in such acts the protection of law and a rationale for enabling moral monsters to hide from themselves. No longer considered "an inadmissible attack on the very idea of humanity"[50] or an attack on the very foundations of justice and democracy, torture in the Bush-Cheney administration was elevated to a state-sanctioned policy and tactic, a pragmatic punishing strategy divorced from moral principles.

President Bush and Vice President Cheney worked tirelessly to ensure that the United States would not be constrained by international prohibitions against cruel and inhumane treatment, and they furthered that project not only by making torture, as Mark Danner, a writer for the *New York Review of Books*, puts it, "a marker of political commitment" but also by constructing a vast secret and illegal apparatus of violence in which, under the cover of national security, alleged terrorists could be kidnapped, made to disappear into secret CIA black sites, turned into ghost detainees removed from any vestige of legality, or secretly abducted and sent to other countries to be tortured. Jane Mayer, a writer for the *New Yorker*, remarks,

> The lawyers also authorized other previously illegal practices, including the secret capture and indefinite detention of suspects without charges. Simply by designating the suspects "enemy combatants," the President could suspend the ancient writ of habeas corpus that guarantees a person

the right to challenge his imprisonment in front of a fair and independent authority. Once in U.S. custody, the President's lawyers said, these suspects could be held incommunicado, hidden from their families and international monitors such as the Red Cross, and subjected to unending abuse, so long as it didn't meet the lawyer's own definition of torture. And they could be held for the duration of the war against terrorism, a struggle in which victory had never been clearly defined.[51]

The maiming and breaking of bodies and the forms of unimaginable pain inflicted by the Bush administration on so-called enemy combatants were no longer seen to violate either international human rights or a constitutional commitment to democratic ideals. The war on terror had reduced governance in the United States to a legalized apparatus of terror that mimicked the very violence it was meant to combat. In the aftermath of 9/11, under the leadership of Bush and his close neoconservative band of advisers, justice took a leave of absence and the "gloves came off." In Danner's words, "The United States transformed itself from a country that, officially at least, condemned torture to a country that practised it."[52]

◇

Torture and the Politics of Historical Amnesia

> The United States participated actively and effectively in the negotiation of the Convention Against Torture.... Ratification of the Convention by the United States will clearly express United States opposition to torture, an abhorrent practice unfortunately still prevalent in the world today.... Each State party is required either to prosecute torturers who are found in its territory or to extradite them to other countries for prosecution.
>
> —*Ronald Reagan*[1]

One measure of the culture of cruelty and punishment is the way in which a government uses language to obscure and hide its crimes against humanity. When evidence of state-sponsored terror surfaced in the events surrounding the torture chambers of Abu Ghraib, Guantánamo, and the Afghan prisons, such acts were largely denounced as the work of a "few bad apples" (a position generally endorsed by the Bush administration and now completely discredited) or dismissed as uncharacteristic of American democracy. The bad apple argument was both a purposeful lie and, for a time, an effective cover-up to protect those at the highest reaches of government who both set policy and provided

19

detailed instructions on how actually to carry out certain abusive practices deemed as torture. As *New York Times* columnist Frank Rich argues, "Torture was a premeditated policy approved at our government's highest levels . . . psychologists and physicians were enlisted as collaborators in inflicting pain; and . . . in the assessment of reliable sources like the FBI director Robert Mueller, it did not help disrupt any terrorist attacks."[2]

When the torture memos of 2002 and 2005 were eventually made public by the Obama administration, clearly implicating the Bush-Cheney regime in torture, they revealed that the United States had been turned into a globalized torture state.[3] Conservative columnist Andrew Sullivan went so far as to claim that "if you want to know how democracies die, read these memos."[4] The memos, written by government lawyers John Yoo, Steven Bradbury, and Jay Bybee, allowed the Central Intelligence Agency (CIA) under the Bush administration to torture alleged Al Qaeda detainees held at Guantánamo and other secret detention centers around the world.[5] They also offered detailed instructions on how to implement ten techniques prohibited in the *Army Field Manual*, including facial slaps, "use of a plastic neck collar to slam suspects into a specially-built wall,"[6] sleep deprivation, cramped confinement in small boxes, use of insects in confined boxes, stress positions, and waterboarding. The latter technique, which has been condemned by democracies all over the world, consists of the individual being "bound securely to an inclined bench, which is approximately four feet by seven feet. The individual's feet are generally elevated. A cloth is placed over the forehead and eyes. Water is then applied to the cloth in a controlled manner [and] produces the perception of 'suffocation and incipient panic.'"[7] The highly detailed, amoral way in which these abuses were defined and endorsed by lawyers from the Office of Legal Council is chilling and reminiscent of the harsh and ethically deprived instrumentalism used by those technicians of death in criminal states such as Nazi Germany. Andy Worthington, the British historian and journalist, suggests that there is more than a hint of brutalization and dehumanization in the language used by the OLC's principal deputy assistant attorney general, Steven G. Bradbury, who wrote a detailed memo recommending

> "nudity, dietary manipulation and sleep deprivation"—now revealed explicitly as not just keeping a prisoner awake, but hanging him, naked except for a diaper, by a chain attached to shackles around his wrists—[as,] essentially, techniques that produce insignificant and transient discomfort. We are, for example, breezily told that caloric intake "will always be set at or above 1,000 kcal/day," and are encouraged to compare this enforced starvation with "several commercial weight-loss programs in the United States which involve similar or even greater reductions in calorific intake" ... and when it comes to waterboarding, Bradbury clinically confirms that it can be used 12 times a day over five days in a period of a month—a total of 60 times for a technique that is so horrible that one application is supposed to have even the most hardened terrorist literally gagging to tell all.[8]

The *New York Times* claimed in an editorial "that to read the four newly released memos on prisoner interrogation written by George W. Bush's Justice Department is to take a journey into depravity."[9] The editorial writer was particularly incensed over a passage written by Jay Bybee, who was an assistant attorney general in the Bush administration at the time and is now a federal judge. As the *Times* pointed out, Bybee "wrote admiringly about a contraption for waterboarding that would lurch a prisoner upright if he stopped breathing while water was poured over his face. He praised the Central Intelligence Agency for having doctors ready to perform an emergency tracheotomy if necessary."[10] Bybee's memo is particularly disturbing, even repugnant, in its disregard for human rights, human dignity, and democratic values, not only describing how the mechanics of waterboarding should be implemented but also providing detailed analysis for introducing insects into confined boxes that held suspected terrorist prisoners. In light of mounting criticism, Bybee has both defended his support of such severe interrogation tactics and further argued that "the memorandums represented 'a good faith analysis of the law' that properly defined the thin line between harsh treatment and torture."[11] Indeed, it seems that Bybee should look carefully at the following judgment pronounced by the American court in Nuremberg to the lawyers and jurists who rewrote the law for the Nazi regime: "You destroyed law and justice in Germany utilizing the empty forms of the legal process."[12]

Liberal writers such as Rachel Maddow and Paul Krugman have been clearly troubled by such acts, though they have ascribed such atrocities exclusively to the politics of the Bush administration.[13] Similarly, in the face of incontrovertible evidence that the American government tortures, many critics across the political spectrum have simply argued that such acts were a radical departure from American democratic and moral ideals, suggesting that torture committed by the CIA and the Pentagon was an historical aberration that was not likely to be repeated. Even the allegedly liberal *New York Times* ran a whitewashed story claiming neither top CIA officials nor senior aides to President Bush were aware of the history of waterboarding as an illegal method of torture before they adopted it as an interrogation technique for suspected terrorists—as if that was a justification to the victims on which it was used.[14] In these liberal narratives, the government's decision to cross over to the dark side has been depicted as the decision of the renegade Bush administration alone and used to reinforce the weak, if not fatally flawed, argument that "in waging the war against terrorism, America had lost its way."[15] But, as Charles Kaiser notes, "ex-CIA director George Tenet—and everyone else in the agency—was [far from] ignorant of the history of waterboarding when they decided to use it while interrogating prisoners after 9/11. Never mind that the United States had prosecuted Japanese interrogators for waterboarding their prisoners, or that such simulated drowning was also the favorite technique of the Gestapo against the Resistance in France."[16] Even the *New York Times* has pointed out that waterboarding was a "well-documented favorite of despotic governments since the Spanish Inquisition" and that it was a practice used under Pol Pot—in fact, one "waterboard was on display at the genocide museum in Cambodia."[17]

What most of the commentaries on the use of water-boarding, even liberal ones, share in their condemnation of torture is a peculiar form of historical amnesia—one ready to rehearse the history of torture in countries other than the United States.[18] In fact, America has a long record of inflicting torture on others, both at home and abroad, although it has never admitted to such acts. Instead, the official response has been to deny this history or do everything to hide such monstrous acts from public view through government censorship, appealing to the state secrecy principle, or deploying a language that buries narratives of extraordinary cruelty in harmless-sounding euphemisms. For example, the CIA's benignly named Phoenix Program in South Vietnam resulted in the deaths of over 21,000 Vietnamese. As maverick academic Carl Boggs argues, the acts of U.S. barbarism in Vietnam appeared both unrestrained and never ending, with routinized brutality such as throwing people out of planes labeled as "flying lessons" or "half a helicopter ride";[19] tying a field telephone wire around a man's testicles and ringing it up was a practice called "the Bell Telephone Hour."[20] Officially sanctioned torture was never discussed as a legitimate concern, but, as indicated by a few well-documented accounts, it seems to be as American as apple pie.[21] As Boggs points out, U.S. torture has deep historical roots:

> History shows that present-day U.S. torture and other similar outlawry has deep roots in the past, the byproduct of an ever-expanding imperial apparatus of control and repression. In hundreds of pages of long-classified but recently-disclosed files, CIA documents alone describe an immense variety of illegal activities: secret holding cells around the world, unlawful detentions without due process, vast surveillance, plots to assassinate foreign leaders, severe interrogation methods. Such outrages are the outgrowth of established patterns rather than deviations from (romanticized) historical norms, integral to the far greater savagery of aggressive warfare. U.S. militarism has routinely embraced criminal behavior sanctioned, more often than not, at the highest levels of Washington officialdom. The CIA torture networks in place across several decades, but only recently a focus of mainstream political concern, represent just one cornerstone of U.S. imperial efforts to maximize its global surveillance, intelligence, and control potential.[22]

Similarly, Noam Chomsky and Edward Herman reported as far back as 1979 that of the "35 countries using torture on an administrative basis in the late 1970s, 26 were clients of the United States."[23] But it would be a mistake to suggest that the history of torture runs only through the American presence in Central America, Vietnam, and later at Guantánamo, Abu Ghraib, and Afghanistan. It also has a long-standing presence domestically, particularly as part of the brutalized practices that have shaped American chattel slavery through to its most recent "peculiar institution," the rapidly expanding prison-industrial complex.[24] The racial disparities in American prisons and criminal justice system register the profound injustice of racial discrimination as well as a sordid expression of racist violence. As the novelist Ishmael Reed contends, this is a prison system "that is rotten to the core ... where torture and rape are regular occurrences and where in some states the conditions are worse than at Gitmo. California prison hospitals are so bad that they have been declared unconstitutional and a form of torture."[25] One of the more recently publicized cases of prison torture involved the arrest of a former Chicago police commander, Jon Burge. He was charged with routinely torturing as many as 200 inmates, mostly African Americans, during police interrogations in the 1970s and 1980s, "in order to force them to falsely confess to crimes they did not commit."[26] One report claims that many of these men were beaten with telephone books and that "cattle prods were used to administer electric shocks to victims' genitals. They were suffocated, beaten and burned, and had guns forced into their mouths. They faced mock executions with shotguns.... One tactic used was known as 'the Vietnam treatment,' presumably started by Burge, a Vietnam veteran."[27] The filmmaker Deborah Davis has documented a number of incidents in the 1990s that amounted to the unequivocal torture of prisoners, and she has argued that many of the sadistic practices she witnessed taking place in the American prison system were simply exported to Abu Ghraib. Commenting on some of the tapes of prison torture and abuse she viewed, she notes:

> It's terrible to watch some of the videos and realize that you're not only seeing torture in action but, in the most extreme cases, you are witnessing young men dying.... Savaged by dogs, electrocuted with cattle prods, burned by toxic chemicals, does such barbaric abuse inside U.S. jails explain the horrors that were committed in Iraq? In one horrific scene, a naked man, passive and vacant, is seen being led out of his cell by prison guards. They strap him into a medieval-looking device called a "restraint chair." ... Sixteen hours later, they release him.... And two hours after that, he dies from a blood clot. The tape comes from Utah—but there are others from Connecticut, Florida, Texas, Arizona—

more than 20 cases of prisoners who've died in the past few years after being held in a restraint chair.[28]

The American Civil Liberties Union (ACLU), along with a number of other human rights organizations including the United Nations, has condemned the use of torture tactics in American prisons. Moreover, as cultural critic Alexander Cockburn has written, "in recent years, the United States has been charged by the United Nations and also by human rights organizations such as Human Rights Watch and Amnesty International with tolerating torture in U.S. prisons, by methods ranging from solitary, 23-hour-a-day confinement in concrete boxes for years on end, to activating 50,000-volt shocks through a mandatory belt worn by prisoners."[29] It has been estimated that "the number of people currently held in long-term solitary confinement in the United States, living for years in 80-square-foot concrete cubes lit by round-the-clock fluorescent light, with little or no human contact" is around 25,000.[30] And as freelance journalist Brandon Keim points out, "The United States is alone among developed countries in using long-term solitary confinement on a regular basis."[31]

The convict lease system and the modern prison-industrial complex have always played a defining role in race relations in the United States, but with the rise of the punishing state, they have become a central feature of American foreign and domestic policy. The apparatus of torture and state terrorism is also alive and well in many of the nation's detention centers and jails holding immigrants. Nina Bernstein, writing for the *New York Times*, points out that since October 2003, over 107 immigrants have died in private prisons, federal centers, and county jails.[32] Many of those who died in detention were refused crucial medical care. Immigration and Customs Enforcement officials have shrouded these deaths in secrecy and have refused to cooperate with journalists and human rights organizations reporting on the deaths. Government officials embarrassed by these deaths have often lied about them in order to cover up a potential scandal.[33] Once again, actions synonymous with abuse, death, and other human rights violations are hidden as part of an order of politics that is more characteristic of authoritarian regimes than a country that makes a claim to democratic ideals.

Even children in the United States are not spared cruel and unusual punishment at the hands of the criminal justice system. Youth are often subjected to intolerable conditions that inflict irreparable harm on their minds and bodies. In a society that invests more in hiring prison guards than teachers and allocates less money for schools than for prisons, it is not surprising that "school officials and the criminal justice system are criminalizing children and teenagers all over the country, arresting them and throwing them in jail for behavior that in years past would have never have led to the intervention of law enforcement."[34] As *New York Times* columnist Bob Herbert observes, the fact that young people are being ushered "into the bowels of police precincts and jail cells" for minor offenses "is a problem that has gotten out of control.... As zero-tolerance policies proliferate, children are being treated like criminals."[35] Egregious examples abound. For instance, "a growing number of cities have taken to ticketing and sometimes handcuffing teenagers found on the streets during school hours [while in] New York City, a teenager caught in public housing without an ID—say, while visiting a friend or relative—can be charged with criminal trespassing and wind up in juvenile detention."[36] In many states, young offenders with psychiatric disorders are now being placed in juvenile correction centers rather than in community programs designed to help them. Joseph Penn, a child psychologist, claims that "jails and juvenile justice facilities are the new asylums."[37] Rather than receive the necessary services and treatment for serious mental illnesses, such as bipolar disorder, many of these children are overmedicated, abused by other inmates, and in some cases subjected to cruel and unusual punishment by staff. In 2008, federal civil rights investigators issued a report in which they documented the use of pepper spray on the "mental health population . . . and recounted how staff members body slammed unruly juveniles, often breaking their bones."[38] One psychologist, charged with the task of monitoring "mental health services in California's juvenile justice system," claimed that "some detainees appeared to be held there for no reason other than that they were mentally ill and the country had no other institution capable of treating them."[39]

As the punishing state becomes more expansive, it has a tendency to criminalize everything in its domain, including schools, which partly explains why so many thousands of youth end up under an increasingly draconian criminal justice system. The sociologist Randall Beger has written that the new security culture in schools comes with an emphasis on "barbed-wire security fences, banned book bags and pagers . . . 'lock down drills' and 'SWAT team' rehearsals,"[40] to say nothing of metal detectors, drug-sniffing dogs, strip searches, and the scanning of genital orifices. The appalling violation of the rights of students was recently revealed in a case before the U.S. Supreme Court, which ruled that the strip search of an eight-year-old girl by school authorities (who forced her to partially disrobe, remove her bra, and shake out her underwear for evidence of ibuprofen) was illegal.[41] As the logic of the market and "the crime complex"[42] frame a number of social actions in schools, students are further subjected to zero-tolerance laws that are used primarily to humiliate, punish, repress, and exclude them.[43] In addition, as more and more schools break down the space between education and juvenile delinquency, substituting penal pedagogies for critical learning and replacing a school culture that fosters a discourse of caring support with a culture of fear and social control, many youth of color in urban school systems are being suspended or expelled from school. Beyond that, they have to bear the terrible burden of being ushered into the dark precincts of juvenile detention centers, adult courts, and even adult prisons. Poor black and Latino male youth are particularly at risk in this mix of demonic representation and punitive modes of control, as they are the primary objects of racist stereotypes as well as a range of disciplinary policies that criminalize their behavior.[44] Such youth are arrested and jailed at rates that far exceed those of their white counterparts.[45] In 2002, although black children made up only 16 percent of the juvenile population in the United States, they accounted for 43 percent of arrests (white youth, by contrast, comprised 78 percent of the population but only 55 percent of arrests).[46] Other statistics reveal African American youth now constitute 41 percent of juveniles sent to detention centers, 46 percent of juveniles sent to prison, and 52 percent of juvenile cases transferred to adult criminal courts.[47] Shockingly, in the land of the free and the home of the brave, a "jail or detention cell after a child or youth gets into trouble is the only universally guaranteed child policy in America."[48]

The overall consequence of these punishing policies is the elimination of intervention programs, which in turn boosts the number of youth in prisons, especially minority youth, and keeps them there for longer periods of time. Moreover, when these young people are placed in adult prisons, they are "five times as likely to be raped, twice as likely to be beaten and eight times as likely to commit suicide than adults in the adult prison system."[49] Juvenile detention centers are not much better. According to Professor Barry Feld, "The daily reality of juveniles confined in many 'treatment' facilities is one of violence, predatory behavior, and punitive incarceration."[50] In some juvenile facilities, young people are abused and tortured in a manner associated with the treatment detainees have received at Abu Ghraib, Guantánamo, and various detention centers in Afghanistan and Iraq. For example, the U.S. Department of Justice reported in 2009 that children at four juvenile detention centers in New York were often severely abused and beaten.[51] The use of excessive force by the staff was indiscriminate and was applied ruthlessly.[52] According to the report, "Anything from sneaking an extra cookie to initiating a fistfight may result in full prone restraint with handcuffs. . . . This one-size-fits-all approach has, not surprisingly, led to an alarming number of serious injuries to youth, including concussions, broken or knocked-out teeth, and spiral fracture [bones broken by twisting]."[53] In one instance, a boy simply glared at a staff member and for that infraction was put into a sitting restraint. His arms were pulled behind his back with such force that his collarbone, which had been previously injured, was broken.[54] It appears that the torture of children takes place not only in the dark precincts of prisons outside the United States but within its borders as well. The model of the prison increasingly appears to influence almost every major institution that affects youth directly—both expanding the culture of cruelty and worsening its effects on young people. Surely, it is difficult not to concede that such practices are a violation of the constitutional guarantee against cruel and unusual punishment.

There is something more at work than expressions of unimaginable terror in Jay Bybee's and Steven Bradbury's statements justifying torture: there is also the attempt to make the suffering of the victim an irrelevant, even absurd, concern. Any vestige of moral responsibility disappears and, along with it, any real understanding of the pain suffered by those labeled as enemy combatants at the hands of a state that makes torture its official policy. Consider another example of this outrageous abuse, coming from Bou Meng (known as Duch), one of the Khmer Rouge prison chiefs on trial in Cambodia for crimes against humanity. Duch was the commandant of Tuol Sleng prison, where it has been estimated that over "14,000 people were tortured and sent to their deaths."[55] Duch claimed that he never visited the "prison's cells and torture chambers, asserting that he was a coward, and that he did not participate in, or even know in detail about the abuse of the prisoners . . . [claiming that] 'I shut my eyes and ears. I did not want to see the reality. . . . I did not allow myself to see or hear.'"[56] The Bush administration shares with the rulers of the Khmer Rouge a complicity with torture and human rights abuses, but the members of the Bush administration most responsible—unlike a leader of one of the most notorious genocidal regimes of the twentieth century—apparently have had no qualms about having a direct hand in scripting detailed methods of torture, and they have yet to voice either self-criticism or regret for their culpability in causing the immense suffering of other human beings. In fact, while appearing on ABC's *This Week,* on February 14, 2010, former vice president Cheney not only admitted that he had sanctioned waterboarding—a practice Attorney General Holder claims is torture—but also took pride in displaying his role as a defender of the United States as a torture state!

What is disturbing about the ideological and moral cover provided for torture and crimes against humanity by various members of the Bush administration is that it was justified both by an incessant appeal to fear and by a barely disguised racism while unabashedly suggesting that torture and torture alone was the only way to deal with those subjected to torture. These horrendous practices found their counterpart in the Bush administration's willingness to disregard civil liberties while arguing that because the United States had such a finely tuned moral compass, there was no ethical or legal violation in inflicting physical and psychological pain upon "them," since "they had to be responsible for their own suffering."[57]

◇

CHAPTER THREE

What Is New About Torture?

In the prisons of urban centers such as Chicago and in the torture chambers of Iraq, Guantánamo, Afghanistan, and other black sites, torture tactics were rarely used to garner intelligence. Torture's primary purpose was to induce inmates and detainees to provide incriminating confessions, often resulting in misinformation—the product of a survival tactic employed by the victims of torture to put a stop to the punishment. Many prisoners at Guantánamo and other places under U.S. control have admitted they were willing to sign anything to get the torture to stop. Some critics have argued that the origins of the Bush-era torture practices were adopted from the so-called Survival, Evasion, Resistance, and Escape program (SERE). This program trained soldiers to resist giving confessions and originated in the Korean War when "the Chinese invented torture techniques whose aim was to force American prisoners of war to make false confessions of participation in war crimes for use in propaganda."[1] Not only did the United States draw from the Chinese model of torture developed in the Korean War, it also appropriated its primary purpose, which, once again, was not to extract valuable military intelligence but to solicit false confessions. Misinformation produced nonetheless actionable information, enabling the manipulation of facts by military and intelligence personnel so as to initiate wars or ratchet them up to the next level. This argument is supported by the heavy emphasis the Bush administration placed on using sensory deprivation and other techniques for imposing psychological abuse on high-ranking captives—practices designed to disorient and elicit confessions.[2] In fact, Bush's torture machine uniquely emphasized placing detainees in extreme isolation, cut off from all communication, while promoting modes of sensory deprivation that often resulted in hallucinations, depression, and even outright madness in some cases.

The Argentinean-born writer Pilar Calveiro relates the story of Muhammad al Madni, who was confined for years in a cell at Guantánamo and "had gone completely mad"; he was often heard to say, "Speak to me, please ... I am depressed ... I need to speak to someone."[3] The International Committee of the Red Cross reported that some detainees "were held in the CIA detention program—which ranged from sixteen months up to almost four and a half years and [some] detainees were kept in continuous solitary confinement and incommunicado detention."[4] In another instance, José Padilla, an American citizen and a suspected Al Qaeda operative, was held in severe isolation in a small cell in a high-security military prison, the U.S. Naval Consolidated Brig, located in Charleston, South Carolina, for forty-three months.[5] Labeled as an enemy combatant and deprived of legal counsel by the Bush administration, Padilla endured brutalizing interrogation techniques that had been used by the Soviets during the Cold War and at that time were appropriately, if ironically, condemned by the United States.

According to investigative journalist and author Jeremy Scahill, the Bush administration expanded the exercise of torture in the military and intelligence communities in order to "produce two things that, it turns out, did not exist: weapons of mass destruction programs in Iraq and cooperation between Al Qaeda and the regime of Saddam Hussein. Pressure to find evidence of both intensified in 2002."[6] He writes:

> Soon, prisoners were being tortured to provide evidence of the Al Qaeda–Saddam link. As Col. Lawrence Wilkerson, former Secretary of State Colin Powell's chief of staff, has stated, the "harsh interrogation in April and May of 2002 . . . was not aimed at pre-empting another terrorist attack on the U.S. but discovering a smoking gun linking Iraq and Al Qaeda." And according to the recent Senate Armed Services Committee report on the treatment of detainees, a former Army psychiatrist, Maj. Charles Burney, has confirmed the charge. "A large part of the time," he told Army investigators, "we were focused on trying to establish a link between Al Qaeda and Iraq and we were not successful. . . . The more frustrated people got in not being able to establish that link . . . there was more and more pressure to resort to measures that might produce more immediate results."[7]

In spite of the mounting evidence that the Bush-Cheney regime was torturing U.S.-held captives, the Bush administration repeatedly denied it had engaged in cruel and unusual punishment. Early on in the Bush years, the public did not know that the U.S. government had legitimated policies sanctioning torture, but there were plenty of hints. After all, the administration had repeatedly indicated that it was no longer going to abide by the Geneva Conventions, parts of which the White House counsel, Alberto Gonzales, recklessly labeled "quaint." As Vice President Dick Cheney had announced as early as September 16, 2001, the United States had indeed crossed over to what he called the dark side.[8] And soon after the attacks of September 11, 2001, Cofer Black, the former head of the CIA's Counterterrorism Center, stated unambiguously before the Senate Intelligence Committee what Mark Danner has called "the most telling pronouncement of the era: 'All I want to say is that there was "before" 9/11 and "after" 9/11. After 9/11 the gloves come off."[9] As Danner makes clear, the gloves that had to be taken off were "laws that forbid torture, that outlaw wiretapping and surveillance without permission of the courts, that limit the president's power to order secret operations and to wage war exactly as he sees fit."[10] Even after Bush admitted to the existence of the CIA torture chambers known as black sites and to the use of waterboarding, and after Cheney later admitted that the government had used "enhanced interrogation techniques" to secure information from high-ranking detainees, Bush refused to admit that torture had become the unspoken law of the land.

As shocking as these denials are in light of the information that is now available—including Obama's release of the torture memos, the previously released report by the International Commission of the Red Cross, and the release of a long-secret 2004 report written by the CIA's inspector general—an even more egregious example of government hypocrisy took place on June 26, 2003, when President Bush made statements endorsing the UN International Day in Support of Victims of Torture. He insisted that "the United States declares strong solidarity with torture victims across the world" and also stated that "torture anywhere is an affront to human dignity everywhere. We are committed to building a world where human rights are respected and protected by the rule of law."[11] In spite of the grandiloquent rhetoric, Bush had already violated on numerous occasions the Geneva and Hague Conventions dealing with the abuse of human rights, as well as the due process clause of the Fifth Amendment to the U.S. Constitution and the Eighth Amendment ban on cruel and unusual punishment. For instance, the Canadian journalist Michelle Shepard tells the story of Dilawar, a twenty-two-year-old taxi driver "[falsely] accused of a rocket attack on an American base"[12] and held as a detainee at Bagram soon after in 2002. Following the guidelines in the torture memos, Dilawar was subjected to a technique called the "common peroneal strike," a painful and crippling blow to the thigh; typically, the technique would not have been used "unless a guard's life was in danger," but during Bush's reign, it was used routinely on detainees.[13] And as Shepard points out, the technique was used on Dilawar with horrendous consequences. Shepard adds:

> For four days in 2002, his outstretched arms were chained to the top of his cell. The soldiers used the technique to keep the prisoners awake and upright, the pressure on the wrists unbearably painful if they slumped down asleep. Five days after his capture, Dilawar was found dead in his cell—the second death in Bagram in two weeks. An autopsy found his legs had been beaten so badly that it looked as if he had been run over by a bus. A military coroner determined that his death was a homicide due to "blunt force injuries to lower extremities complicating coronary artery disease."[14]

Further indications of the moral hypocrisy and moral degradation that became official policy under the Bush administration surfaced with the May 30, 2005, Bradbury memo and the 2004 CIA inspector general's report on treatment of terrorist detainees. As mentioned in the memo, Abu Zubaydah was waterboarded 83 times in August 2002, and Khalid Sheikh Mohammed was waterboarded 183 times in March 2003.[15] Mohammed's waterboarding occurred only two months before Bush insisted that "the suffering of torture victims must end, and the United States calls on all governments to assume this great mission"[16]—this from a President who ordered illegal kidnappings to be cleverly called "renditions," who lied about weapons of mass destruction to justify the ill-fated invasion of Iraq, who turned America into a state that tortures, who authorized secret assassination squads, who officially permitted indefinite detention of U.S. captives by labeling them as enemy combatants, who legally sanctioned the suspension of habeas corpus for prisoners, and who created military commissions in which individuals can be proven guilty on the basis of hearsay and unproven accusations.

The CIA secret report written by the agency's inspector general in 2004 and released under a court order in 2009 documented the degree to which the Bush administration's torture tactics had gone far beyond waterboarding. According to the report, CIA interrogators threatened to use a power drill on Abd Al-Rahim Al-Nashiri, a detainee who was hooded and naked. They also placed an unloaded semiautomatic handgun next to his head and threatened to shoot him. Interrogators then staged a mock execution nearby, suggesting that the same fate awaited Al-Nashiri if he did not talk. But the descent into barbarism did not end there. Al-Nashiri was also told that if he did not talk, CIA interrogators would bring in his mother and other family members—the implication being they would be tortured and sexually abused in front of the detainee. Other incidents outlined in the report included threats to kill a detainee's children; beating a detainee with a rifle butt; and inducing hypothermia by putting detainees in diapers, dousing them with cold water, and then subjecting them to extremely cold temperatures. Another detainee was choked by interrogators who put excessive pressure on his carotid artery until he became unconscious.[17] There is more reflected here than the violation of federal laws against torture or exposure of the brutal treatment of detainees at the hands of military and CIA interrogators. There is also what investigative reporter Dave Lindorff calls the "unnecessary and totally criminal descent into barbarism." Lindorff writes:

> We've got a litany of horror and abuse here that sounds like the worst kind of stories that used to come out of Saddam Hussein's Iraq, or the Argentine Junta or Idi Amin's Uganda. About the only thing missing is the word that the military

and CIA torturers were eating their victims, or feeding them their own genitals, but who knows? Maybe we'll get there yet. It's hard at this point to rule anything out. What has become of the US?[18]

Under the Bush-Cheney administration, a number of distinctive features emerged that suggested there were significant differences in the way the government was using torture as compared to its previous history in this arena. One of the major indicators that torture was embraced in unprecedented ways was the fact that the government, despite President Bush's 2003 speech, seemed less eager to suppress and more eager to show off, frequently and forcefully, its no-holds-barred approach to the war on terror. Recall Bush's claim in 2002 that the United States would no longer be constrained by the Geneva Conventions' prohibitions against cruel and inhumane treatment regarding Al Qaeda or Taliban detainees, violating with impunity the 1948 universal ban on torture and deviating from "the rest of the democratic international community."[19]

In the past, a careful dividing line had been demarcated and maintained between what was made public regarding the treatment of prisoners of war and what took place behind closed doors. U.S. participation in torture was both hidden and often exported to regimes in Central and Latin America as well as Asia. Americans supplied the advice, training, and education in moral degradation, and others did the dirty work. On the surface at least, the U.S. government denounced torture carried out by its enemies while secretly promoting torture and human rights abuses among those dictatorships considered friendly to its interests. Luke Mitchell, a senior editor at *Harper's Magazine,* gets it right with his comment: "This was the age of hypocrisy—our secrecy was the tribute war crimes paid to democracy."[20] British lawyer and author Phillipe Sands, in an interview with Bill Moyers, claimed that what was new was "the abandonment of the rules against cruelty ... in order to clear the slate and allow aggressive interrogation."[21] According to Sands, the abandonment of the military tradition that refused to participate in evil acts gave way to what he has called a "culture of cruelty." He states:

> It slipped into a culture of cruelty. There was, as it was put very pithily for me by a clinical psychologist, Mike Gellers, who is with the Naval Criminal Investigation Service, spending time down at Guantánamo, who described to me how once you open the door to a little bit of cruelty, people will believe that more cruelty is a good thing. And once the dogs are unleashed, it's impossible to put them back on. And that's the basis for the belief amongst a lot of people in the military that the interrogation techniques basically slipped from Guantánamo to Iraq, and to Abu Ghraib.[22]

One register of the transformation at every level of power toward a culture of cruelty was revealed in the Abu Ghraib photos, in which the torturers actually included themselves. As Pilar Calveiro writes, "The inclusion of the perpetrators, smiling and victorious within the photographic frame [suggested] they seem proud to be torturers, which would represent an authentic innovation in the self-representation of the redressed [who] in the past never recognized himself as a torturer, but rather used euphemisms to describe his 'work,' and tended to think of himself as a kind of technician carrying out a disagreeable but necessary function."[23] Another register of the simultaneous expansion and self-legitimation of the culture of cruelty can be found in the ways in which torture became "clean," making barbarous violations on the body and psyche less traceable and visible as markers of cruelty and state-sponsored pain. As renown historian of torture Darius Rejali makes clear, the lingua franca of torture now involves "clean techniques" or what he calls "clean torture"—such as stress positions, loud noise, extreme temperatures, isolation, drugs, electricity, and threats against family—all of which leave no visible marks of abuse.[24]

But there is another element to how torture is both represented and, despite its concreteness and specificity, ignored. When pundits and critics talk about torture, those defending it reveal not merely an indifference to ethics, suffering, and human rights but also a hardness, an emotional callousness, as part of what Frankfurt School theorist Theodor Adorno has called a "thingified consciousness"— which makes barely conscious the monstrosity of practices such as torture. For Adorno, this is not just a psychological problem; it is also a social issue deeply tied to a culture that lacks public values, denies compassion, and promotes a cutthroat competitiveness that "represents an unfree form that tends towards violence."[25] In a neoliberal society where compassion is a liability and images of militarized masculinity fuel popular culture, brutality and violence become markers of individual and national identity that all too easily legitimate forms of masochism and sadism as acceptable social practices. As the larger culture is emptied of democratic values, institutional practices, disciplinary technologies, and visual culture sanction and mediate a culture of cruelty. Needless to say, this is both a political issue and a pedagogical one—an issue in which market-based values and institutions of power combine with wider educational forces to give the daily rituals of hypermasculinity, militarism, violence, and psychic hardness a stylish appeal and normative legitimacy.

There appears to be an endless stock of snapshots of this hardness and indifference to human life that are brought to light with increasing frequency daily—Gilded Age excesses combining an indifference to mass poverty and growing homelessness, anger expressed at the social state, racist discourse on talk radio, public apathy to the growing army of the unemployed, and hysteria emanating from the ranks of right-wing fundamentalists. But on occasion, the door opens wide and a particular type of barbarism is briefly revealed that signals something less ritualistic and more disturbing about the social and political fabric of American culture. One such incident took place not too long ago when John Yoo, one of the Bush administration's most influential legal architects, had a public exchange with international human rights scholar Doug Cassel. Referring to Yoo's 2002 memo, Cassel posed a question to Yoo:

Cassel: If the President deems that he's got to torture somebody, including by crushing the testicles of the person's child, there is no law that can stop him?
Yoo: No treaty.
Cassel: Also no law by Congress. That is what you wrote in the August 2002 memo.
Yoo: I think it depends on why the President thinks he needs to do that.[26]

Yoo's comments reflect a psychology devoid of any ethical sensibility, appearing willfully indifferent to the violence done in the name of unaccountable government authority and also willing to look away when evidence of practiced torture, unimaginable cruelty, and state-sanctioned terrorism could no longer be denied. But Yoo's answer is also disturbing because it reveals the connections between the hardened masculinity and militarism of the culture at large and a state-sanctioned legal violence in which sadism finds a comfortable footing. As a vocal advocate of the torture state, Yoo exemplifies a culture of cruelty capable of producing both an egregious perversion of justice and what it means to be a human being.

As repulsive as Yoo's position is, it was echoed in different terms in March 2003 when the *Wall Street Journal* ran a story entitled "How Do U.S. Interrogators Make a Captured Terrorist Talk?" In one particularly disturbing paragraph, Jess Braven and Gary Fields write: "U.S. authorities have an additional inducement to make Mr. Mohammed talk, even if he shares the suicidal commitment of the Sept. 11 hijackers: The Americans have access to two of his elementary-school-age children, the top law enforcement official says. The children were captured in a September raid that netted one of Mr. Mohammed's top comrades, Ramzi Binalshibh."[27] The implication that the United States is justified in torturing these children in order to make the father talk is presented uncritically in one of the most important newspapers in the United States, indicating the degree to which children have been devalued and the culture of cruelty has been both normalized and reduced to the uncritical status of common sense.

Another example of the type of ethical and psychic hardening that enables this kind of human cruelty and abuse is revealed in a memo dated November 27, 2002, in which Defense Secretary Donald Rumsfeld approved a series of interrogation techniques as part of an effort to put more pressure on captive U.S. detainees. One of the techniques called for having detainees stand for up to four hours. Rumsfeld objected to the four-hour restriction and scrawled a short note: "I stand for 8–10 hours a day. Why is standing limited to 4 hours? D. R."[28] Mark Danner, commenting on Rumsfeld's remark, speaks powerfully to the culture of cruelty that the former secretary of defense both embodied and helped produce. Danner observes:

> Secretary Rumsfeld, who no doubt was standing at his desk when he scrawled these words, professed to have difficulty comprehending the difference between working at a standing desk in one's office—signing documents, talking on the telephone, speaking to subordinates, drinking coffee—and standing naked in a very cold room with hands shackled to the ceiling for hours and days at a time.... After 18 to 24 hours of continuous standing, there is an accumulation of fluid in the tissues of the legs. This dependent edema is produced by the extravasation of fluid from the blood

vessels. The ankles and feet of the prisoner swell to twice their normal circumference. The edema may rise up the legs as high as the middle of the thighs. The skin becomes tense and intensely painful. Large blisters develop, which break and exude watery serum.[29]

Evidence of this type of psychic hardening and moral depravity extends far beyond the torture memos and the triumphalist justifications for imperial power that fuel Rumsfeld's comments. Even after President Obama condemned torture and made it illegal once again, those politicians and lawyers who supported torture and played a prominent role in both legitimating it and sanctioning it under the Bush administration refused to exhibit the slightest bit of self-reflection or remorse over their support for a state that tortures. For instance, in a revealing interview with Deborah Solomon of the *New York Times,* James Inhofe, a conservative Republican senator from Oklahoma, stated that he did not think the naval base at Guantánamo should be closed because it was "a real resource."[30] Inhofe then talked about Gitmo, this gulag for the stateless roundly condemned all over the world, as if it were a vacation spot generously provided by the U.S. government for detainees who in actuality were legally but unjustly rendered as part of America's war on terror. What is even more astounding is that Inhofe seemed completely unwilling to entertain the overwhelming and substantial body of evidence that proves many of the detainees at Guantánamo were subjected by the American government to sexual abuse, human rights violations, and the systemic practice of torture. He stated, without any irony intended: "The people there are treated probably better than they are in the prisons in America. They have more doctors and medical practitioners per inmate. They're eating better than anyone has ever eaten before.... One of the big problems is they become obese when they get there because they've never eaten that good before."[31]

There is more than denial and ignorance at work in In-hofe's answers. They are also symptomatic of a society that is no longer capable of questioning itself, unraveling its ability to think critically and act in a morally responsible way. This is a society in which moral claims are no longer open to examination, and the consequences spell catastrophe for democracy. In another interview, Solomon asked John Yoo, the former Justice Department lawyer and one of the architects of the torture memos, if he regretted writing those memos, which offered President Bush a legal rationale for ignoring domestic and international laws prohibiting torture.[32] Exhibiting a complete indifference to the moral issue at stake in justifying systemic torture, Yoo gave an answer not unlike those provided by Nazi war criminals prosecuted at the Nuremberg military tribunals in 1945. He stated: "No, I had to write them. It was my job. As a lawyer, I had a client. The client needed a legal question answered."[33]

Rumsfeld, Inhofe, Yoo, and too many others to name exhibit and legitimate the type of unethical behavior that is chilling and surely reflects the fundamental political and moral corruption at the heart of the Bush and Cheney administration. But the cruelties and crimes that these individuals and that administration produced as official policy could not have taken place if there was not a formative culture in place in the United States that both supported and enabled such acts of barbarism to be committed against thousands of people. Within such a culture, as Judith Butler reminds us, it becomes increasingly easy for human life to be sacrificed to an instrumental logic, a totalitarian view of authority, and a discourse of fear. Such a culture loses its moral compass, sanctions policies of cruelty and disposability, and in the end becomes unable to entertain those norms or shared conditions that make human life possible, that apprehend the dignity of human life or offer the political and moral frameworks "to guard against injury and violence."[34] Under such circumstances, individual rights, protections, and civil liberties disappear as the most barbaric state-sanctioned practices are carried out with only minor opposition registering among the American people. The culture of cruelty that emerges in this context speaks not merely to the death of public values or to a society that is politically adrift but more importantly to the demise of democracy itself.

Chapter Four

The Disappearing Body

In June 2005, Vice President Dick Cheney, in response to revelations of torture at Guantánamo, claimed that the prisoners in the detention camp inhabited something similar to Club Med. According to Cheney, "They're living in the tropics. They're well fed. They've got everything they could possibly want."[1] What is most scandalous about this remark is not the sheer duplicity of the misrepresentation or even the trivialization of human rights violations but the attempt to silence an ever-expanding narrative of extreme cruelty and pain inflicted on the bodies of those who have been forced to inhabit, without any legal rights, what would be more aptly called Club Torture.

We know from a number of reports and from the leaked images of Abu Ghraib prison that enemy combatants in various detention centers have been subjected to the most horrendous forms of torture, often severely injured and left to suffer with irreparable mental anguish. In other instances of torture and abuse, detainees "have been murdered."[2] Renowned blogger and lawyer Glenn Greenwald claims that "at least 100 detainees in U.S. custody have died since 2002, many suffering gruesome deaths."[3] Scott Horton, writing for *Harper's Magazine,* asserts that three prisoners who the U.S. government alleged had killed themselves in June 2006 may have died not from suicide but from torture.[4] One of the three men, Yasser Talal Al-Zahrani, was only seventeen years old when he was captured and interned at Guantánamo. When presented with a copy of his son's suicide note, Tal Al-Zahrani, a former brigadier general in the Saudi police force, said, "'This is a forgery.'"[5] According to Horton, Al-Zahrani also stated that when viewing his son's corpse, "'there was evidence of torture on the upper torso, and on the palms of his hand. There were needle marks on his right arm and on his left arm.' None of these details are noted in the U.S. autopsy report. 'I am a law enforcement professional,' Al-Zahrani said. 'I know what to look for when examining a body.'"[6] In spite of inconsistencies in the camp commander's story, the testimony of some guards at the camp who saw all three detainees being taken to the secret black site at Guantánamo known as Camp No, and new autopsy evidence uncovered by Horton—all of which suggested "that the three men were suffocated and tortured during questioning" at the black site—the Obama administration has refused to investigate the case.

According to the Center for Constitutional Rights (CCR), many prisoners at Guantánamo have been

> held in solitary confinement for periods that exceed a year; deprived of sleep for days and weeks and, in at least one case, months; exposed to prolonged temperature extremes; beaten, sexually harassed and raped or threatened with rape; deprived of medical treatment for serious conditions, or allowed treatment only on the condition that they "cooperate" with interrogators; and routinely "short-shackled" (wrists and ankles bound together to the floor) for hours and even days during interrogations.[7]

Moreover, the CCR states that some detainees were held in solitary confinement for more than a year or two and that many of them, such as Saber Lahmar and Belkacem

Bensayah, have "suffered visual deterioration and psychological trauma as a result."[8] It also reports that many detainees kept in isolation were confined and shackled in rooms under the glare of fluorescent lights for twenty-four hours a day and for as long as three years in some cases. As if the confinement and shackles were not enough, many also had to endure loud music continually pumped into their cells. We get a glimpse of this type of abuse from an FBI interrogator who documented the combined use of sleep deprivation and very cold temperatures on detainees. He writes:

> On a couple of occasions, I entered interview rooms to find a detainee chained hand and foot in a fetal position to the floor, with no chair, food, or water. Most times they had urinated or defecated on themselves, and had been left there for 18, 24 hours or more. On one occassion [*sic*], the air conditioning had been turned down so far and the temperature was so cold in the room, that the barefooted detainee was shaking with cold.... On another occasion, the A/C had been turned off, making the temperature in the unventilated room probably well over 100 degrees. The detainee was almost unconscious on the floor with a pile of hair next to him. He had apparently been literally pulling his own hair out throughout the night.[9]

In another instance, as described in the CCR report, the detainee, Mr. Al Murbati, was interrogated in a room whose temperature was moved purposefully between extreme cold or hot. And for several days, Al Murbati was doused with a mixture of water and a powerful cleaning agent, which caused great irritation to his face and body. And as the CCR report points out, on several occasions

> he was shackled to the floor by his hands and feet, with his hands pulled underneath his legs. For approximately 12 hours, very loud music and white noise was played through

six speakers arranged close to Mr. Al Murbati's head.... In certain sessions, multiple flashing strobe lights were used as well; these lights were so strong that Mr. Al Murbati had to keep his eyes closed. The interrogation rooms were always cold when the music and strobe lights were employed.[10]

One detainee describes the experience of being left alone in a room while being shackled and bombarded with strobe lights and loud music. He states:

You lose track of time ... after a while—because you're confined to a really small room, you're tied down into this position, they've got the stereo banging out really loud with strobe lights flashing like ten times a second—it makes you hallucinate. At the beginning it doesn't really affect you. But after a while, after like 20 minutes, 10 minutes, you start getting cramps in your thighs, and your buttocks, and your calves, and slowly your legs, you know, just go numb. You're flimsy, and you've got no control. And when you move over, [the shackles] start cutting into you.... And even if you close your eyes you can still see the light and you start hallucinating.... Sometimes you'd get punched or kicked as well.[11]

Many detainees have also reported numerous incidents of vicious beatings and physical abuse. Sami Al-Laithi claims that military guards stomped on his back and broke two of his vertebrae. He is now confined to a wheelchair. He says, "I am in constant pain. I would prefer to be buried alive than continue to receive the treatment I receive. At least I would suffer less and die."[12] According to one chilling description provided by the Center for Constitutional Rights, Lakhadar Boumediene was subjected on several occasions to the following abuse:

In early 2002 when guards returned him to his cell following interrogation, [they] grabbed him under his armpits, lifted him up, and threw him to his cage floor repeatedly while his wrists were shackled to his waist and his feet were shackled to an anchor in the floor of his cage.... And on one occasion, a soldier pushed him to the ground, put his knee behind Mr. Boumediene's knee, and ground Mr. Boumediene's knee into the floor. He now has a scar he attributes to that beating."[13]

As mentioned previously, one of the most deplorable examples of torture committed as a result of policies initiated by the Bush administration is the waterboarding of detainees. Cheney and his army of government lawyers refused to acknowledge, under the cover of illegal legalities, that the drowning method is an act of torture and a human rights violation—in spite of it being outlawed by democratic nations throughout the world. As noted earlier, Abu Zubaydah, currently in U.S. custody in Guantánamo, was waterboarded eighty-three times in August 2002. As detailed in a Red Cross report, he describes the process as follows:

After the beating I was then placed in the small box. They placed a cloth or cover over the box to cut out all light and restrict my air supply. As it was not high enough even to sit upright, I had to crouch down. It was very difficult because of my wounds. The stress on my legs held in this position meant my wounds both in the leg and stomach became very painful.... I was then dragged from the small box, unable to walk properly and put on what looked like a hospital bed, and strapped down very tightly with belts. A black cloth was then placed over my face and the interrogators used a mineral water bottle to pour water on the cloth so that I could not breathe. After a few minutes the cloth was removed and the bed was rotated into an upright position. The pressure of the straps on my wounds was very painful. I vomited. The bed was then again lowered to horizontal position and the same torture carried out again with the black cloth over my face and water poured on from a bottle. On this occasion my head was in a more backward, downwards position and the water was poured on for a longer time. I struggled against the straps, trying to breathe, but it was hopeless. I thought I was going to die. I lost control of my urine. Since then I still lose control of my urine when under stress. I was then placed again in the tall box. While I was inside the box loud music was played again and somebody kept banging repeatedly on the box from the outside. I tried to sit down on the floor, but because of the small space the bucket with urine tipped over and spilt over me.... I was then taken out and again a towel was wrapped around my neck and I was smashed into the wall with the plywood covering and repeatedly slapped in the face by the same two interrogators as before. I was then made to sit on the floor with a black hood over my head until the next session of torture began. The room was always kept very cold.[14]

Yet another one of the most shameful acts from Abu Ghraib also known to be used at Guantánamo was the alarming application of techniques designed to sexually humiliate and degrade prisoners. One instance was widely reported in the press: "Female interrogators tried to break Muslim detainees at the U.S. prison camp at Guantánamo Bay by sexual touching, wearing a miniskirt and thong underwear and in one case smearing a Saudi man's face with fake menstrual blood."[15] Stories abound in both the media and in official reports about female interrogators performing "strip club lap dances" on Muslim detainees, parading in front of them wearing bikinis and lingerie while sexually taunting them, and in some cases offering sexual favors in exchange for information. As a result of this abuse, many detainees have tried to commit suicide, and on June 10, 2006, three of them were found dead in their cells. Others have undertaken hunger strikes in protest and as a result had to endure forced feedings.[16] All these practices are evidence of torture and cruel, inhuman, and degrading treatment routinely experienced by detainees at Guantánamo Bay—hardly the Club Med vacation Vice President Cheney suggested.

Under the Obama administration, hundreds of detainees continue to be deprived of their legal rights and are subjected to inhumane treatment at Bagram air base, the main American detention center in Afghanistan. Held as "unlawful combatants," these detainees do not even have the legal rights afforded to prisoners at Guantánamo Bay.[17] Afghan detainees can defend themselves before military commissions but are not granted access to legal counsel. The Associated Press recently reported that in July 2009, "hundreds of prisoners [at Bagram] are refusing privileges such as recreation time and family visits in protest at their lack of legal rights."[18]

The utter disregard for legal rights and the sanctioning of cruel and unusual punishment are also taking place inside the United States, involving dozens of terrorist cases subject to post–9/11 measures that are now being tried in the federal courts. One egregious example concerns the case of Syed Mehmood Hashmi, a "U.S. citizen, born in Pakistan and raised in Flushing, Queens."[19] As he was about to board a plane in London's Heathrow Airport, he was seized by passport control and then extradited to the United States. Hashmi's crime, according to the U.S. government, is that while he was a graduate student in London in 2004, he allowed "an acquaintance from Queens," who stayed with him for a few weeks, to stash luggage at his London apartment. Unfortunately for Hashmi, the luggage contained what the government labeled "military gear" for Al Qaeda, consisting of "a bunch of raincoats and waterproof socks." Hashmi was charged with "aiding someone who was aiding terrorists" and now faces seventy years in prison.[20] As freelance writer Petra Bartosiewicz points out, "Much of the evidence against him is secret, and he can't see it because he doesn't have a security clearance."[21] Even his lawyer cannot see a good deal of the evidence. In the meantime, Hashmi is locked in a "Special Housing Unit at the Metropolitan Correctional Center."[22] According to Bartosiewicz,

Today Hashmi, who is 29, sits in a windowless cell, in solitary confinement. He is not allowed to watch television or listen to the radio or read a newspaper unless it is at least 30 days old and censored. He is not allowed to speak to guards, other inmates, or the media, or to write anyone but his attorney and his family (once a week on three single-sided pages). The only people cleared to visit, besides his lawyer, are his mother and father, but he couldn't see them for three months after he was caught shadowboxing in his cell—an infraction that cost him visiting privileges. Hashmi's lawyer, Sean Maher, says the isolation is slowly driving his client mad.[23]

What is truly deplorable about the "secret" justice and cruel and unusual punishment being meted out in cases such as Hashmi's is that it is not taking place under an administration that prides itself on subverting civil liberties and sanctioning torture but under the liberal presidency of Barack Obama. It seems that the dark shadow of Gitmo extends far beyond the shores of Cuba, tainting any claim to justice and democracy by an administration that has formally condemned the use of torture by the Bush administration.

Torture destroys the capacity for speech, voice, and dignity. It also destroys the law, makes a mockery of justice, and empties democracy of any substance. It reduces power to a blunt and brutalizing instrument that seeks (mis) information, producing mostly false confessions and the scandal of a national self-deceit that operates as a kind of self-sabotage regarding an alleged commitment to democratic values.[24] But, of course, it does more. When torture becomes legalized, it moves the radical evils of sadism and ideological certainty from the margins to the center of American domestic and foreign policy. What is new here and cannot be forgotten is that legal violence and the state of exception no longer occupy the periphery of legal discourse, social relations, or domestic and foreign policy: they are now defining elements of a new American authoritarianism and exceptionalism. The last few decades have witnessed the transformation of a democratic state (albeit imperfect) into a punishing state at home and a warrior state abroad. What unites these two horrific manifestations of the new American law and order is the normalization of torture and the racial definition of its victims.

◇

Chapter Five

The Unthinkable

Torturing Children

The media machine loves violence, terror, and every other conceivable catastrophe for the spectacle they provide and the audience ratings they attract. In a culture of cruelty, spectacularized violence is matched by the rhetoric of verbal combat. Utilization of a militaristic language, suffused with images of warfare and violence, represents the new communicative norm. Dialogue has now been replaced by heated argument, and verbal exchanges resemble assassination attempts against an enemy. As Professor Warren Sack argues, "We 'attack' our opponents' positions and 'defend' our own. We 'shoot down' opposing arguments. We say that claims are 'defensible' or 'indefensible.' We talk of 'winning' and 'losing' arguments.... We are 'on target' or 'off target' in our criticisms. We 'gain ground' or 'lose ground.' In fact, it is not simply that we talk about arguments like this, this is what we do."[1]

Might this suggest that addressing each other as enemies makes it all the more easy to inhabit and construct a culture of violence that traffics in pain, just as it obliterates any moral obligation to care for the other? Australian sociologist Peter Beilharz suggests, "Just as we as individuals

57

feel no responsibility towards the other, so does the sense of political responsibility for social problems weaken."[2] Without such a brutalizing language and culture, it might be more difficult to inhabit a society in which the suffering of others is endlessly reducible to empty entertainment, providing a representational anchor for how little we regard the value of human life and what we have become as a nation. The traffic in pain has now become so embedded in everyday life that we barely acknowledge it. Professors Mark Reinhardt and Holly Edwards insist, "This traffic is a crucial element of news reporting, obviously, but it also courses through the art market, tourism, even fashion and advertising. Without injured bodies and devastated landscapes, without scenes of death, destruction, misery, and trauma, the contemporary image environment would be nearly unrecognizable."[3]

In this spectacularizing of violence and pain, even the suffering of young people fails to compel responsibility and is either trivialized or ignored. Nowhere is there a more disturbing, if not horrifying, example of the relationship between a culture of cruelty and the politics of irresponsibility than in the resounding silence that surrounded the torture of children under the presidency of George W. Bush—and the equal moral and political failure of the Obama administration to address and rectify the conditions that made it possible. But if we are to draw out the dark and hidden parameters of such crimes, they must be made visible so men and women can once again refuse to orphan the law, justice, and morality. Young people both at home and abroad often have to endure the most harsh brutalities, and when they resist, they are often punished, especially if they are underprivileged youth. Poor minority, immigrant, and working-class youth in the age of unbound market forces have been removed from the world of ethical concerns and social responsibility and recast in the image of society's fears and dangers. Excised from the language of compassion and deprivation, they are now defined as part of the discourse of depravity and pathology.[4] But it is difficult to demonize children when they are victims of torture, and it is equally difficult not to raise issues about the responsibility of adults who look the other way when it happens. How we deal with the issue of state terrorism and its complicity with the torture of children will determine not only the conditions under which we are willing to live but also whether we will live in a society in which moral responsibility disappears altogether and we come to find ourselves existing under an authoritarian social order. This is a political and ethical matter but also a matter of how seriously we take the task of educating ourselves more critically in the present, for the sake of a more democratic future.

We have not always looked away. When Emmett Till's battered, brutalized, and broken fourteen-year-old body was open to public viewing in Chicago after he was murdered in Mississippi in 1955, his mother refused to have him interred in a closed casket. His mutilated and swollen head, his face disfigured and missing an eye, made him unrecognizable as the young, handsome boy he once was. The torture, humiliation, and pain this innocent African American youth endured at the hands of white racists was transformed into a sense of collective outrage and pain, and this helped launch the civil rights movement. Torture when inflicted on children reveals itself in its lurid, revolting reality, defying the very conditions for its justification. Even among those who believe that torture is a defensible practice to extract information, the case for inflicting pain and abuse upon children proves impossible to support. The images of young children being subjected to prolonged standing, handcuffed to the top of a cell door, doused with cold water, raped, and shocked with electrodes boggle the mind and shatter thought. Corrupting and degenerate practices, such despicable acts also reveal the utter moral depravity underlying the rationales used to defend torture as a viable war tactic.

There is an undeniable pathological outcome when the issue of national security becomes more important than the survival of morality itself, sometimes resulting in the deaths of thousands of children that raise not even a public murmur. For instance, former secretary of state Madeleine Albright, appearing on the national television program *60 Minutes* in 1996, was asked by Leslie Stahl for her reaction to the killing of half a million Iraqi children as a result of the five-year-long U.S. blockade. Stahl pointedly asked her, "We have heard that a half million children have died. I mean, that's more children than died in Hiroshima. And, you know, is the price worth it?" Albright replied, "I think this is a very hard choice, but the price—we think the price is worth it."[5] The comment was barely reported in the mainstream media and produced no outrage among the American public. As blogger and author Rahul Mahajan points out, "The inference that Albright and the terrorists may have shared a common rationale—a belief that the deaths of thousands of innocents are a price worth paying to achieve one's political ends—does not seem to be one that can be made in the U.S. mass media."[6] More recently, Professor Michael Haas has argued that in spite of the ample evidence that the United States has both detained and abused what may be hundreds of children in Iraq, Afghanistan, and Guantánamo, there has been almost no public debate about the issue and precious few calls for prosecuting those responsible for the torture. He states:

> The mistreatment of children is something not so funny that has been neglected on the road to investigations of and calls for prosecution of those responsible for torture. George W. Bush has never been asked about the abuse of children in American-run prisons in the "war on terror." It is high time for Bush and others to be held accountable for what is arguably the most egregious of all their war crimes—the abuse and death of children, who should never have been

arrested in the first place. The best kept secret of Bush's war crimes is that thousands of children have been imprisoned, tortured, and otherwise denied rights under the Geneva Conventions and related international agreements. Yet both Congress and the media have strangely failed to identify the very existence of child prisoners as a war crime.[7]

Although it is difficult to confirm how many children were actually detained, sexually abused, and tortured by the Bush administration, there is ample evidence that such practices took place. Reuters columnist Sherwood Ross cites Human Rights Watch, which estimated in June 2008 that up to 513 juveniles were being detained in U.S. custody. He also points to the claims of a renowned journalist who estimated that "800–900 Pakistani boys aged 13 to 15" were being held as detainees.[8] Ralph Lopez, founder of Jobs for Afghans, provides a compilation of additional evidence of the alleged torture of children, including testimony from Thaar Salman Dawod, a former detainee, who said in a witness statement, "[I saw] two boys naked and they were cuffed together face to face and [a U.S. soldier] was beating them and a group of guards were watching and taking pictures and there was three female soldiers laughing at the prisoners."[9] Also significant is former president Jimmy Carter's claim that the Red Cross, Amnesty International, and the Pentagon "have gathered substantial testimony of the torture of children, confirmed by soldiers who witnessed or participated in the abuse" and that as many as 107 detainees, "some as young as eight years old," were found by the Red Cross after visiting six U.S. prisons.[10] In the summer of 2004, Seymour Hersh, one of America's most prominent journalists and a reporter for the *New Yorker,* gave a speech to the ACLU in which he charged that children were sodomized in front of women in a prison while some guards filmed the horrendous violation and that the Pentagon has a tape of it. After this shocking revelation, he further claimed that the worst things that took place at Abu Ghraib have yet to be revealed. According to a transcript of his remarks, Hersh reported the following:

> Debating about it, ummm.... Some of the worst things that happened you don't know about, okay? Videos, um, there are women there. Some of you may have read that they were passing letters out, communications out to their men. This is at Abu Ghraib.... The women were passing messages out saying "Please come and kill me, because of what's happened" and basically what happened is that those women who were arrested with young boys, children in cases that have been recorded. The boys were sodomized with the cameras rolling. And the worst above all of that is the soundtrack of the boys shrieking that your government has. They are in total terror. It's going to come out.[11]

Numerous reports by journalists have substantiated Hersh's account and even provided further evidence confirming the torture and sexual abuse of children in the various detention centers under the control of U.S. forces. The *Telegraph* in England reported that thirteen former detainees at Abu Ghraib made statements in which they claimed that "an Iraqi boy was raped in custody and that other inmates were threatened with death and made to retrieve food from toilets."[12]

In May 2004, German television broadcast a documentary report titled *Iraq: One More Sin—Evidence of Children Being Abused in Abu Ghraib,* written by Thomas Reutter. Reutter interviewed Sgt. Samuel Provance, a U.S. Army intelligence officer, who provided the following statement about the torture of a sixteen-year-old boy he led to an interrogation session at Abu Ghraib. He writes:

> He was full of fear, very alone. He had the thinnest little arms that I have ever seen. His whole body shook. His wrists were so thin that we could not put handcuffs on him.

As soon as I saw him for the first time and led him to the interrogation, I felt sorry for him. The interrogation specialists doused him with water and put him in a truck. Then they drove with him through the night, and at that time it was very, very cold. Then they smeared him with mud and showed him to his likewise imprisoned father. [The interrogation team] had tried out other interrogation methods. But they had not succeeded in making him talk. The interrogation specialists told me that after the father had seen his son in that condition it broke his heart. He wept and promised to tell them what they wanted to know.[13]

Reutter also interviewed Suhaib Badr-Addin al-Baz, an Iraqi television journalist who was imprisoned in Abu Ghraib for seventy-four days. According to al-Baz, he not only saw over 100 children imprisoned at the facility but also heard a twelve-year-old girl crying in a nearby cell after she had been beaten and stripped naked. He reported that he also heard her shouting, "They undressed me! They poured water over me!"[14] Jonathan Steele wrote in the *Guardian* that "hundreds of children, some as young as nine, are being held in appalling conditions in Baghdad's prisons, sleeping in sweltering temperatures in overcrowded cells, without working fans, no daily access to showers, and subject to frequent sexual abuse by guards, current and former prisoners say."[15] He cites the case of sixteen-year-old Omar Ali, who "spent more than three years in the Karkh juvenile prison" and who told Steele that "he was able to shower only once every three days," that he slept in a cell just 5 by 10 meters with seventy-five other boys, and that "guards often [took] boys to a separate room in the prison and rape[d] them."[16] In his book *George W. Bush, War Criminal?* Michael Haas documents in great detail various crimes, abuses, and forms of torture committed against children in Iraq, Guantánamo Bay, and Afghanistan under policies initiated by the Bush administration.[17] He argues that the United States has committed a number of war crimes in violation of the rights of children, including placing children in solitary confinement while in prison, denying children the right to have contact with their parents, abdicating the responsibility to protect children from acts of abuse including rape, using dogs to deliberately frighten them, denying them any form of education, and shackling them in painful positions.[18] He also cites numerous specific examples of brutalization and torture, such as the case of "an ill 15-year-old who was forced to run up and down Abu Ghraib with two heavy cans of water and beaten whenever he stopped. When he finally collapsed, guards stripped and poured cold water on him. Finally, a hooded man was brought in. When unhooded, the boy realized that the man was his father, who doubtless was being intimidated into confessing something upon sight of his brutalized son."[19]

As far back as April 2003, the U.S. military admitted that children as young as sixteen were among those held as detainees at the prison camp at Guantánamo Bay.[20] Some of the detained children had been imprisoned for more than a year, sparking outrage among a number of human rights groups. A military spokesman claimed that the children were being held because "they have potential to provide information in the ongoing war on terrorism [and] their release is contingent on the determination that they are not a threat to the nation and have no further intelligence value."[21] What is shocking about this comment is that it stands in violation of the legal status of such youths and willfully ignores that the evacuation, imprisonment, and torture of children is a breach of the Geneva Conventions, the Conventions on the Rights of the Child (CRC), and numerous other related international agreements, all of which accentuate the need to accord special protection and rights to children.

In spite of the military acknowledging that children were held at Guantánamo, the U.S. government refused initially to comment on whether it detained children in U.S.-controlled detention centers. But this was later confirmed at a press conference in May 2003, when Donald Rumsfeld admitted that the United States held juveniles—even as he simultaneously tried to invalidate their status, if not humanity, as children. In an attempt to echo the Bush administration's penchant for blurring the legal distinction between children and adults, he stated, without the slightest hint of either shame or self-reflection: "This constant refrain of 'the juveniles,' as though there's a hundred children in there—these are not children." His comments were later followed by an even more callous response to the presence of children at the prison by Gen. Richard Myers, the chairman of the Joint Chiefs of Staff. Myers remarked that "[they] may be juveniles, but they're not on the Little League team anywhere. They're on a major league team, and it's a terrorist team, and they're in Guantánamo for a very good reason—for our safety, for your safety."[22] Myers simply echoed a central assumption of the Bush administration, held with certainty, that anyone named as an enemy combatant—a status unrecognized by international law—now inhabited a wild zone of imperial power, a space in which the state of exception prevailed, depriving individuals of any rights whatsoever, presupposing their guilt, and dismissing the possibility of their innocence. But what Myers made clear for the first time was that this legal illegality now applied not only to adults but also to children.

As media reports surfaced about juveniles being held at Guantánamo and other U.S.-run detention centers, a Pentagon spokesman, Lt. Cmdr. Jeffrey Gordon, defying all semblance of reason and indifferent to international law, claimed that under the rules of war, age was simply not a matter of consideration in detaining suspected terrorists. According to Gordon, "There is no international standard concerning the age of individuals who engage in combat operations. Age is not a determining factor in the detention [of those] engaged in armed conflict against our forces or in support to those fighting against us."[23] Gordon appeared unaware that on February 6, 2003, the United States ratified the Optional Protocol to the Conventions on the Rights of the Child on the Involvement of Children in Armed Conflict, which labels a child as someone under eighteen years old and further stipulates that anyone under that age is a victim of war, not a war criminal.[24] Moreover, the CRC also labels as a war crime the evacuation of children to another country as well as the failure of a state to notify the parents of children who are taken into custody. As mentioned earlier, Michael Haas has documented a number of instances in which war crimes were committed against children by the U.S. forces, including the placing of children "in the same prison alongside adults at Abu Ghraib, where rapes were reported of both male and female children."[25]

Journalist Cori Crider reveals that in May 2008, a Pentagon report issued to the United Nations "said that no more than eight youths, aged 13 to 17 at time of capture, were held at Guantánamo Bay. But a prisoner list released in 2006 in response to a U.S. Freedom of Information Act lawsuit names 21 inmates under 18 when they arrived. A separate defense department admission brings the total to 22. Testimonies collected by the charity Reprieve, which represents 30 inmates at Guantánamo, indicate the actual number is much higher."[26] This does not include, of course, the hundreds of children held in U.S.-run detention centers in Iraq and Afghanistan. While recognizing that the Bush administration disputed the following numbers, Haas claims that in 2008, the administration "reported to the UN-assisted Committee on the Rights of the Child that the United States from 2002 had detained 2,400 children in Iraq and 100 in Afghanistan, though another source claims that the figure for Afghanistan is 800. As of May 2008, there were 21 at Guantánamo. That month, the Committee upbraided the United States for charging minors with war crimes instead of treating underage persons as victims of war."[27] From a moral and ethical standpoint, the fetishization of numbers misses the point; whether there were 50 or 500, the absolute inhumanity of the act remains unchanged. And even if Americans were to abide by the perilous and irresponsible claim that their security would be undermined by releasing the detained children, what has become clear since the statements made by Rumsfeld and General Meyers is that many of the detainees, including the children, imprisoned in U.S.-controlled centers are actually there by mistake.

As far back as February 2004, a report issued by the International Committee of the Red Cross stated that "certain [Coalition Forces] military intelligence officers told the ICRC that in their estimate between 70 percent and 90 percent of the persons deprived of their liberty in Iraq had been arrested by mistake."[28] The study also concluded that "the arrest and detention practices employed by U.S.-led forces in Iraq 'are prohibited under International Humanitarian Law.'"[29] It should not surprise anyone familiar with the history of American militarism that the U.S. government has on occasion detained, disappeared, and tortured innocent people. What is truly shocking and unfathomable is that the United States, by disregarding international laws that make legal distinctions between adults and children, now applies the same illegal and barbarous and abusive practices to children as young as eleven years old.

Information and evidence regarding the sexual abuse, torture, and violation of children's rights by the United States under the Bush administration also emerged in a number of legal documents. For instance, the *New York Times* reported that Clive A. Stafford Smith, a London-based human rights lawyer, said "his client, [M. C.], a Saudi of Chadian descent, was not yet 15 when he was captured and has told him that he was beaten regularly in his early days at Guantánamo." According to the *Times,*

The details of M. C.'s accusations are contained in a 17-page account prepared by Mr. Stafford Smith, in which the prisoner said that he was suspended from hooks in the ceiling for hours at a time with his feet barely missing the floor, and that he was beaten during those sessions. M. C. said a special unit known as the Immediate Reaction Force had knocked out one of his teeth and later an interrogator burned him with a cigarette. Mr. Stafford Smith said he saw the missing tooth and the burn scar. Some of M. C.'s descriptions match accounts given not only by other detainees, but also by former guards and interrogators who have been interviewed by the *New York Times*. He describes being shackled close to the floor in an interrogation room for hours with music blaring and lights in his face. He also said he was shown a room with pictures of naked women and adult videos and told he could have access if he cooperated. His description fits the account of former guards who described such a room and said it was nicknamed "the love shack."[30]

Some of the most extensive documentation of the torture of children comes from a number of reports dealing with the cases of three of the most famous child detainees—Omar Khadr, Mohammed El-Gharani, and Mohammed Jawad—all of whom were juveniles upon arrest and were transferred by U.S. forces to Guantánamo Bay, Cuba. As of August 2009, Khadr remains imprisoned there. Deemed to be "adults," all have faced trials by military commissions and then U.S. courts, making clear that the Obama administration is following the Bush regime's disregard for the Geneva Conventions and the rights of children.

Omar Khadr is a Canadian citizen who was detained in Afghanistan in July 2002 at the age of fifteen, following a four-hour battle in which it is alleged he threw a grenade that killed a U.S. soldier.[31] Even though he was seriously wounded, Khadr's torture began soon after he was captured. According to one report,

Omar Khadr's torture began almost as soon as he was taken to Bagram Air Force Base in Afghanistan after his capture, in July of 2002. Although badly wounded during his capture, Omar's interrogation began even as he lay in recovery, days after his arrival at the hospital with nearly mortal wounds. He was carried on a cot to an interrogation room and denied pain medication until he cooperated. Weeks later, he was forced to carry heavy buckets of water up and down the halls at Bagram, solely to aggravate his slowly healing body, and he was hung from the door sill by wrist shackles for hours as a disciplinary measure for talking in his cell.[32]

While at Bagram, Khadr claims that he was interrogated "42 times in 90 days" and that "on other occasions, interrogators threw cold water on me.... On several occasions at Bagram, interrogators threatened to have me raped, or sent to other countries like Egypt, Syria, Jordan or Israel to be raped.... Many times, during the interrogations, I was not allowed to use the bathroom, and was forced to urinate on myself."[33] In violation of international law, Omar Khadr was transferred around October 28, 2002, to the detention center at Guantánamo. He was sixteen years old. He describes the trip as follows:

> For the two nights and one day before putting us on the plane, we were not given any food so that we would not have to use the bathroom on the plane. They shaved our heads and beards, and put medical-type masks over our mouths and noses, and goggles and earphones on us so that we could not see or hear anything. One time, a soldier kicked me in the leg when I was on the plane and tried to stretch my legs. On the plane, I was shackled to the floor for the whole trip. When I arrived at Guantánamo, I heard a military official say, "Welcome to Israel." They half-dragged half-carried us so quickly along the ground off the plane that everyone had cuts on their ankles from the shackles.

> They would smack you with a stick if you made any wrong moves.[34]

It gets worse. After young Omar Khadr arrived at Guantánamo, he was often placed in solitary confinement, interrupted only for interrogations that occurred under horrendous conditions and included being hooded and threatened with barking dogs. How is national security safeguarded by putting a teenage boy in strict conditions of isolation with no possibility of human contact (except, of course, when he is tortured), no voices to communicate with, no conversations with other human beings, "no tapping out messages on the walls, [n]o ability to maintain a sense of human connection, a sense of place or time"?[35] Such isolation techniques constitute cruel and unusual punishment and were banned by the *Army Field Manual.* Michael Haas states that Khadr "has also been administered a brutal beating while on a hunger strike, threatened with rape, and denied pain medication."[36] One of the most cruel depictions of the torture inflicted on this young boy is documented in an affidavit he provided to Amnesty International, in which Khadr describes how he was used as a human mop. He states:

> The interrogator became extremely angry, then called in military police and told them to cuff me to the floor. First they cuffed me with my arms in front of my legs. After approximately half an hour they cuffed me with my arms behind my legs. After another half hour they forced me onto my knees, and cuffed my hands behind my legs. Later still, they forced me on my stomach, bent my knees, and cuffed my hands and feet together. At some point, I urinated on the floor and on myself. Military police poured pine oil on the floor and on me, and then, with me lying on my stomach and my hands and feet cuffed together behind me, the military police dragged me back and forth through the mixture of urine and pine oil on the floor. Later, I was put back in my

cell, without being allowed a shower or change of clothes. I was not given a change of clothes for two days. They did this to me again a few weeks later.[37]

Another child, Mohammed El-Gharani, a citizen of Chad, was just fourteen years old when he was arrested in Pakistan in 2001 and handed over to the United States in 2002. Andy Worthington claims that El-Gharani was "treated with appalling brutality" once he was in the custody of U.S. forces. He writes:

> After being tortured in Pakistani custody, he was sold to U.S. forces, who flew him to a prison at Kandahar airport, where, he said, one particular soldier "would hold my penis, with scissors, and say he'd cut it off." His treatment did not improve in Guantánamo. Subjected relentlessly to racist abuse, because of the color of his skin, he was hung from his wrists on numerous occasions, and was also subjected to a regime of "enhanced" techniques to prepare him for interrogation—including prolonged sleep deprivation, prolonged isolation and the use of painful stress positions—that clearly constitute torture. As a result of this and other abuse, including regular beatings by the guard force responsible for quelling even the most minor infractions of the rules, El-Gharani has become deeply depressed, and has tried to commit suicide on several occasions.[38]

The evidence against El-Gharani bordered on the surreal. According to U.S. military interrogators, El-Gharani, while living in Saudi Arabia and only eleven years old, joined up with an Al Qaeda cell based in London, England. Equally ridiculous is the fact that these accusations came exclusively from other detainees at Guantánamo, with no outside confirmation. In February 2009, a U.S. district judge ordered the boy's release, stating that "the Justice Department failed to prove that Mohammed El-Gharani, 21, is an enemy combatant because it relied heavily on statements made by other detainees whose credibility is questionable."[39]

In December 2002, another child, Mohammed Jawad, was captured in Afghanistan after he allegedly threw a hand grenade at a military vehicle and injured an Afghan interpreter and two U.S. soldiers. He was immediately arrested by the local Afghan police, who tortured him and consequently elicited a confession from him. In a letter to the U.S. government, an Afghan attorney general claimed that Jawad was twelve years old when captured, indicating that he was still in primary school, though other sources claim he was around fifteen or sixteen.[40] Jawad denies the charges made by the Afghan police, stating that "they tortured me. They beat me. They beat me a lot. One person told me, 'If you don't confess, they are going to kill you.' So, I told them anything they wanted to hear."[41] On the basis of a confession obtained through torture, Jawad was turned over to U.S. forces and detained first at Bagram and later at Guantánamo. This child, caught in the wild zone of permanent war and illegal legalities, has spent more than six years as a detainee. Unfortunately, the Obama administration, even after admitting that Jawad had been tortured illegally, has asked the court to detain him so that it can decide whether or not it wants to bring a criminal charge against him. After a federal judge claimed the government's case was "riddled with holes," the Obama administration decided it would no longer consider Jawad a "military detainee but [that he] would be held for possible prosecution in American civilian courts."[42]

This shameful decision was made contrary to any reason or modicum of morality and justice. Even Jawad's former military prosecutor, Lt. Col. Darrel Vandeveld, a Bronze Star recipient, has stated that there "is no credible evidence or legal basis" to continue his detention and that he does not represent a risk to anyone.[43] In an affidavit filed with the ACLU, he claimed that "at least three other Afghans had been arrested for the crime and had subsequently confessed, casting considerable doubt on the claim that Mr. Jawad was solely responsible for the attack."[44] Vandeveld also pointed out that the confession obtained by the Afghan police and used as the cornerstone of the Bush case against Jawad could not have been written by him because "Jawad was functionally illiterate and could not read or write [and] the statement was not even in his native language of Pashto."[45] The ACLU points out that "the written statement allegedly containing Mohammed's confession and thumbprint is in Farsi," which Jawad does not read, write, or speak.[46] Vandeveld was so repulsed by the fact that all the evidence used against the boy was forcibly obtained through torture that he "first demanded that Jawad be released, then, when Bush officials refused, unsuccessfully demanded to be relieved of his duty to prosecute and then finally resigned."[47] He is now a key witness in Jawad's defense and works actively with the ACLU to get him released. As Bob Herbert has written, "There is no credible evidence against Jawad, and his torture-induced confession has rightly been ruled inadmissible by a military judge. But the administration does not feel that he has suffered enough."[48] And yet, Jawad was the subject of egregious and repugnant acts of torture from the moment he was captured in Afghanistan and later turned over to American forces.

In a sworn affidavit, Colonel Vandeveld stated that Jawad had undergone extensive abuse at Bagram for approximately two months: "The abuse included the slapping of Mr. Jawad across the face while Mr. Jawad's head was covered with a hood, as well as Mr. Jawad's having been shoved down a stairwell while both hooded and shackled."[49] As soon as the boy arrived at Bagram, the abuse began with him being forced to pose for nude photographs and undergo a strip search in front of a number of witnesses. He was also blindfolded and hooded while interrogated and "told ... to hold on to a water bottle that he believed was actually a bomb that could explode at any moment." In addition, while in the custody of U.S. forces, he was subjected to severe abuse and torture. According to the ACLU:

> U.S. personnel subjected Mohammed to beatings, forced him into so-called "stress positions," forcibly hooded him, placed him in physical and linguistic isolation, pushed him down stairs, chained him to a wall for prolonged periods, and subjected him to threats including threats to kill him, and other intimidation. U.S. forces also subjected Mohammed to sleep deprivation; interrogators' notes indicate that Mohammed was so disoriented at one point that he did not know whether it was day or night. Mohammed was also intimidated, frightened and deeply disturbed by the sounds of screams from other prisoners and rumours of other prisoners being beaten to death.[50]

The specifics of the conditions at Bagram under which Jawad was confined as a child are spelled out in a military interrogator's report:

> While at the BCP [Bagram Collection Point] he described the isolation cell as a small room on the second floor made of wood.... He stated that while he was held in the isolation cells, they kept him restrained in handcuffs and a hood over his head, also making him drink lots of water. He said the guards made him stand up and if he sat down, he would be beaten.... [He] stated that he was made to stand to keep him from sleeping and said when he sat down the guards would open the cell door, grab him by the throat and stand him up. He said they would also kick him and make him fall over, as he was wearing leg shackles and was unable to take large steps. He said the guards would fasten his handcuffs to the isolation cell door so he would be unable to sit down.... [He] said due to being kicked and beaten at the BCP, he experienced chest pains and difficulty with urination.[51]

The interrogations, abuse, and isolation daily proved so debilitating physically and mentally that Jawad told military personnel at Bagram he was contemplating suicide. What must be kept in mind is that this victim of illegal abuse and torture was only a juvenile, still in his teens and not even old enough to vote in the United States.

Unfortunately, the torture and abuse of this child continued as he was transferred to Guantánamo. Starved for three days before the trip and given only sips of water, he arrived in Cuba on February 3, 2003, and was subjected to physical and linguistic isolation for thirty days—the only human contact being with interrogators. In October 2003, he underwent another thirty-day period of solitary confinement. The interrogators displayed a ruthlessness with this young boy that is hard to imagine, all in the absence of legal counsel for Jawad. "Military records from throughout 2003 indicate that Mohammed repeatedly cried and asked for his mother during interrogation. Upon information and belief, before one interrogation, Mohammed fainted, complained of dizziness and stomach pain, but was given an IV and forced to go through with the interrogation."[52] Driven to despair over his treatment, Jawad attempted suicide on December 25, 2003.

Hints of such despair had been observed by one interrogator, who approached a military psychologist and said that the "techniques being applied to Jawad should be temporarily halted because they were causing him to dissociate, to crack up without providing good information."[53] These techniques were particularly severe, and as political blogger Meteor Blades points out, they can cause "physical deterioration, panic, rage, loss of appetite, lethargy, paranoia, hallucinations, self-mutilation, cognitive dysfunction, disorientation and mental breakdowns, any of which, alone or in combination, can spur the detainee to give interrogators more information than he might otherwise surrender."[54] Army lieutenant colonel Diane

M. Zeirhoffer, a licensed psychologist, refused to stop the abuse, which she had ordered, and beyond that, according to the testimony of Lieutenant Colonel Vandeveld, she also engaged in a psychological assessment "[not to] assist in identifying and treating any emotional or psychological disturbances Mr. Jawad might have been suffering from [but] instead conducted to assist the interrogators in extracting information from Mr. Jawad, even exploiting his mental vulnerabilities to do so.... From my perspective, this officer had employed his or her professional training and expertise in a profoundly unethical manner."[55] This is a profoundly egregious example of how the war on terror, its reign of illegal legalities, and its supportive culture of cruelty transforms members of a profession who take an oath to "do no harm" into military thugs who use their professional skills in the service of CIA and military interrogations and detainee torture—even the almost unspeakable torture of juveniles.

The abuse of Jawad, bordering on Gestapo-like sadism, continued after his attempted suicide. From May 7 to 20, 2004, he was subjected to what military interrogators called the frequent flyer program, which, as noted earlier, is a systematic regime of sleep disruption and deprivation. In order to disrupt his sleep cycle, Jawad, according to military records, "was moved between two different cells 112 times, on average every two hours and 50 minutes, day and night. Every time he was moved, he was shackled."[56] As a result of this abuse, "Mohammed's medical records indicate that significant health effects he suffered during this time include blood in his urine, bodily pain, and a weight loss of 10% from April 2004 to May 2004."[57] At a June 2008 military commission hearing, Jawad's U.S. military lawyer inquired as to why "someone in a position of authority ... and not just the guards" was not being held accountable for the boy's subjection to the frequent flyer program.[58] The government refused to supply any names or prosecute anyone involved in the program, citing their right to privacy, as if such a right should override "allegations of torture or other cruel, inhuman or degrading treatment or punishment and the right of victims of human rights violations to remedy."[59]

The torture and abuse of the child detainee continued up to the end of 2008. Jawad was further subjected to "excessive cold, loud noise, prolonged linguistic isolation and prolonged exposure to excessively bright lights," and on or about June 2, 2008, he was "beaten, kicked, and pepper-sprayed while he was on the ground with his feet and hands in shackles, for allegedly not complying with guards' instructions. Fifteen days later, there were still visible marks consistent with physical abuse on his body, including his arms, knees, shoulder, forehead, and ribs."[60] How the Obama administration could possibly defend building a criminal case against Mohammed Jawad, given that he was under eighteen years old at the time of his arrest and has endured endless years of torture and abuse at the hands of the U.S. government, raises serious questions about the ethical and political integrity of this administration and its alleged commitment to human rights.

The case against this young man was so weak that Judge Ellen Segal Huvelle not only accused the government of "dragging [the case] out for no good reason" but also expressed alarm at the weakness of the government's case, stating in a refusal to give them an extension to amass new evidence against Jawad, "You'd better go consult real quick with the powers that be, because this is a case that's been screaming at everybody for years. This case is an outrage to me. . . . I am not going to sit up here and wait for you to come up with new evidence at this late hour. . . . This case is in shambles."[61] On July 30, 2009, Judge Huvelle ordered the Obama administration to release Jawad by late August. She stated, "After this horrible, long, tortured history, I hope the government will succeed in getting him back home. . . . Enough has been imposed on this young man to date."[62] The *New York Times* reported, in what can only be interpreted as another example of bad faith on the part of the Obama administration, that the Justice Department responded initially to Judge Huvelle's ruling by suggesting that "they were studying whether to file civilian criminal charges against Mr. Jawad. If they do, officials say, he could be transferred to the United States to face charges, instead of being sent to Afghanistan, where his lawyers say he would be released to his mother."[63] After holding the young boy for almost seven years, the Obama administration freed him on August 24, 2009, and had him flown home to Afghanistan.

Forced to free Jawad after a federal judge said the case was full of holes, the Obama administration still refused to admit that the boy had been tortured or illegally held captive by U.S. forces, even though he was a juvenile when arrested. Shamefully, the Justice Department issued a statement after Jawad's release that claimed, "The criminal investigation of Jawad is still open but his transfer back to Afghanistan makes prosecution unlikely."[64] Further impugning the Obama administration's unwillingness to admit the government's moral and legal violations in the Jawad case are disturbing statements made by Jawad's defense lawyers, who claimed that the witnesses used in bringing a criminal case against their client were paid by the government for their testimony. According to U.S. Marine Corps major Eric Montalvo, one of Jawad's lawyers, all of the alleged witnesses "received some sort of U.S. government compensation, from shoes and a trip to the United States to $400 for cooperation, which is a princely sum in Afghanistan."[65] This type of moral deception and sleazy illegality is straight from the playbook of high-level Republican operatives in the Bush-Cheney administration. Moreover, this type of practice, with Jawad and other detainees, highlights the contradiction between Obama as an iconic symbol of a more democratic and hopeful future and the reality of an administration that is capable of reproducing some of the very worst policies of the Bush administration. Jawad's case is about more than legal incompetence; it is also about the descent into the dark side where a culture of cruelty reigns, the law is on the side of the most frightening of antidemocratic practices, and a society of terror becomes as totalizing as the loss of any sense of ethical responsibility. The U.S. government's reliance on torture, especially of a child, would appear to have more in common with the techniques used by the Gestapo, Pol Pot, Idi Amin, the Pinochet thugs in Chile, and the military junta in Argentina in the 1970s rather than with the United States—or at least the democratic country the United States has historically claimed itself to be.

The culture of cruelty and state terrorism merge in horrifying and indefensible ways when children are tortured, forced to give confessions, held indefinitely without legal representation, refused special education privileges, and denied the rights guaranteed in any viable democracy. With the Bush administration's torture of children, the use of state power in the service of that end lost all semblance of credibility in claiming that such barbarous practices kept Americans safe from terrorists; that they were necessary to punish monstrous wrongdoers who were less than human and "only understand violence"; or that they could prevent the "ticking bomb" scenario, which of course was not, unfortunately, only the stuff of Fox programming fantasy.[66] What are we to make of the argument that Guantánamo contains the "worst of the worst" when we have not only released hundreds of innocent detainees but imprisoned in blatant violation of the Geneva Conventions children who are not yet old enough to get a driver's licence in the United States?

Militarism breeds a warrior mentality and hardened masculinity and also spawns a culture of fear and a willed amorality that can countenance the ugliest of crimes against humanity. (Never mind the hysteria produced by right-wing ideologues who trade in fearmongering and offer a quick resort to violence to solve the nation's problems.) Even the dominant media have supported both the U.S. government's right to torture and its unwillingness to prosecute those responsible for such abuses.[67] On such occasions, the ruthlessness and criminal nature of this type of culture become obvious. Consider when Chris Matthews, host of the MSNBC program *Hardball,* said in an exchange with U.S. senators Saxby Chambliss and Ben Nelson:

> Well, let me ask you, Senator Nelson, should we execute these people? I mean, let's be honest about it. If we believe they're evil, if we believe they're coming to get us—they're hardened killers and terrorists and they intend, the minute they get out, to come back and try to kill us—why are we so dainty about it? Why do we keep holding them? Why don't we execute them? I mean, isn't this just passing the buck, continually saying, "Where do we put these people," when we really think they're our enemies and always will be?[68]

As this comment suggests, we diminish ourselves as a country by elevating the legitimacy of torture to one of the central issues of our time. Beyond that, we further sanction the logic of state violence by suggesting that we can simply murder people we suspect might be terrorists. In this scenario, civil liberties, justice, human dignity, and a sense of civic and moral responsibility become liabilities, unsuited to our desire to normalize torture or to establish the legal and pedagogical conditions, as Darius M. Rejali puts it in a different context, that allow the American people to "relate to torture as a familiar event of modern life."[69] If torture is relegated to the status of common sense, its relationship to producing, if not legitimating, a crime as horrendous as state-sanctioned murder appears to be completely erased from any discussion of torture in the United States.

Widespread political and media support for either promoting torture or not holding accountable those responsible for it has also had a profound effect on public opinion. Well over half the people support the use of torture under certain circumstances "and do not want to see an investigation of Bush administration officials who authorized harsh interrogation techniques on suspected terrorists, even though most people think such procedures were forms of torture."[70] As Glenn Greenwald rightly argues, "Just think about what that says about how coarsened and barbaric our populace is and what types of abuses that entrenched mentality is certain to spawn in the future."[71] It is not difficult to see how pro-Bush ideologues, given the culture of cruelty in which they are situated, would barely notice either the false premises of the torture debate or the ways in which such arguments are used to produce policies in which children now become targets of state violence and victims of torture. The United States in its fascination with market branding has now tragically and immorally taken on the cruel and unlikely designation of the torture state, a name that not only redefines and lessens America's standing around the world but also diminishes any claims the country might make to supporting, if not embodying, democratic ideals (thoroughly problematic before the Bush administration but now unapologetically disparaged).

Under the Bush administration, the United States, imbued with a mix of arrogance and criminality, presented a new version of itself to the rest of the world. No longer a model for the ideals of equality, freedom, justice, and democracy, it consolidated its power under an imperial presidency and a compliant Congress so as to mimic authoritarian regimes such as the old Soviet Union and the former military juntas in Chile and Argentina. We also know, as Andrew Sullivan points out, that the president of the United States and his closest advisers devised, orchestrated and monitored interrogation methods banned by the Geneva Conventions at Guantánamo Bay and subsequently in every theater of combat; these techniques were used not only in the extra-legal no-man's land of Guantánamo Bay but also at the prison at Abu Ghraib where photographic evidence of many of the actual techniques explicitly authorized by the president—stress positions, hoods, mock-executions, etc.—was incontrovertible. We now know that those techniques that the president expressed "shock" at were already explicitly authorized for use by other agents by him long before Abu Ghraib was exposed.[72]

Under the reign of the punishing state and the culture of cruelty, methods that were once prosecuted by the United States as war crimes are now used by the CIA and the Pentagon, even under the Obama administration. People continue to be "disappeared," denied the right of habeas corpus, thrown in military prisons, tortured, held in custody indefinitely, and in some cases murdered.

◊

Chapter Six

Bush's Legacy and Obama's Challenge

Democracy expresses itself in a continuous and relentless critique of institutions; democracy is an anarchic, disruptive element inside the political system; essentially, a force for *dissent* and change. One can best recognize a democratic society by its constant complaints that it is *not* democratic enough.

—*Zygmunt Bauman*[1]

Under the rule of Bush and Cheney, America lost its moral compass as a nation by making torture a premeditated policy legitimated at the highest levels of government. Furthermore, it sanctioned the mental and physical abuse of children—a war crime that the media and American public even in a post-Bush era refuse to acknowledge fully. Under such circumstances, the United States appears to have given up on what it means to question itself critically, take responsibility for actions carried out in its name, and promote notions of justice and basic human rights that affirm the dignity of others. In violating human rights, destroying hard-won civil liberties, elevating the unacceptable obscenity of torture to a national policy, and subjecting both adults and children to unimaginable pain and suffering, it combined a notion of political power and military might that made a mockery of justice, international law, and ethical responsibility. As the United States moved to the dark side, it shed any pretense to either innocence or morality and sacrificed any claim it might make "as a symbol and example of a democratic way of life."[2] American democracy did not merely prove that it was fragile or that it had lost its capacity to be self-reflective—it became overtly dysfunctional as the Bush administration moved to drain it of any moral substance, all the while making a hypocritical appeal to democratic principles to justify its authoritarian practices. The move to the dark side was accompanied by the abuse of government power, eschewing responsibility under the appeal to national security, a culture of fear, and an unwavering belief in the power of American exceptionalism. A will to violence and self-deception now promoted state policies under which the war on terror produced a terrorizing dehumanization of anyone arbitrarily deemed by the Bush administration as an enemy combatant and held captive as an involuntary resident of the state of exception.

Barack Obama assumed the presidency of the United States with the legacy of Bush's crimes casting a long shadow over his administration. Obama provided a symbol of hope, seizing the public imagination with the promise of regime change and a better life. At the same time, he "preached the gospel of peace and hope and carefully avoided making lavish promises."[3] As a presidential candidate, he had spoken with principle and conviction about not sacrificing democratic values to national security, and he criticized both Guantánamo and state-sanctioned torture as violations of human rights and international laws that had to be corrected if the United States was to undo its shameful reputation and amend its grievous political standing in the world. And, in fact, soon after he assumed the presidency, he promised to close Guantánamo, ban the practice of torture, close down the CIA black sites, and limit the state secrets privilege. But President Obama's lofty rhetoric has been overtaken by a certain backtracking, characterized as "cautiousness," that keeps this administration stuck in reverse.

Unfortunately, Obama's rousing and nimble rhetoric of hope quickly lost its luster and credibility as it was increasingly decoupled from a range of policies that suggested the Democratic Party had no intention of parting ways with traditional Center-Right politics. With billions of taxpayer dollars given to the major banks, financial institutions, and auto companies, Obama made it clear that the Democratic Party was still the favored party of finance capital and expanding militarism. But Obama did more than simply bail out the rich; he also violated his own call for "America to speak out on behalf of human rights, and tend to the light of freedom, and justice, and opportunity, and respect for the dignity of all peoples."[4] Rather than ending the illegal legalities and nightmarish approach to national security instituted by the Bush administration and speak and act in the name of moral authority, Obama appears to be legitimating, if not extending, many of the policies he inherited when he took office. For example, he has since defended the idea of preventive detention, which allows the government to imprison people for years without giving them access to any legal rights. He not only wants to revive military commissions but also has supported the state secrets privilege, a favorite tool of the Bush administration. Actually, Obama has outdone the Bush administration on the latter issue by arguing in a Supreme Court filing that "the state secrets privilege was rooted in the Constitution"—making it all the more difficult for Congress to modify it.[5] Obama's belief that the U.S. government can suppress evidence, undermine the Freedom of Information Act, and weaken government transparency by invoking national security is not simply a "pure manifestation of the Bush mentality"[6] but also a threat to any viable notion of democracy. As Glenn Greenwald argues:

> [The] critical issue here is whether the President should have the power to conceal evidence about the Government's actions on the grounds that what the Government did was so bad, so wrong, so inflammatory, so lawless, that to allow disclosure and transparency would reflect poorly on our country, thereby increase anti-American sentiment, and thus jeopardize The Troops. Once you accept that rationale—the more extreme the Government's abuses are, the more compelling is the need for suppression—then open government, one of the central planks of the Obama campaign and the linchpin of a healthy democracy, becomes an illusion.[7]

Obama appears to have emptied the rhetoric of hope of any substance by turning his back on many of the promises he made during his presidential campaign. His notion of hope has been decoupled from any sense of human rights, moral urgency, or civic courage. As blogger Adam Serwer points out, it is hard to take Obama's language of hope or commitment to human rights seriously in light of his "adopting a politics of indefinite detention, suppressing evidence of torture, feeding amendments that would expand PATRIOT Act powers through his political enemies, and embracing a hybrid legal system for suspected terrorists based on the strength of the government's case rather than the nature of the crime."[8]

One of the most telling violations of civil liberties committed by the Obama administration is its blocking of the release of forty-four photos of American soldiers engaged in various acts of detainee abuse in Iraq and Afghanistan. This stance especially echoes the antidemocratic principles of the Bush administration, which was more than willing to sacrifice political values and the integrity of the law in the name of national security. By refusing to release photos of those tortured by U.S. forces, Obama sadly continues yet another element of the Bush regime organized around an attempt to regulate the visual field and to mandate what can be seen as part of an effort to modify the landscape of the sensible and visible. Equally important, as Judith Butler argues in a different context, the Obama administration's refusal to give the victims of torture any recognition or public voice grants the government the power to determine "which lives count as human and as living, and which do not."[9] This is especially troubling when some of these suppressed images involve the torture of children, an issue that should not be hidden from the American public.

Obama and his defenders argue that releasing the inflammatory torture photos would reflect badly on the United States, increasing anti-American sentiment around the world and putting the lives of American troops in jeopardy. According to Obama, "The publication of these photos would not add any additional benefit to our understanding of what was carried out in the past by a small number of individuals.... In fact, the most direct consequence of releasing them, I believe, would be to further inflame anti-American opinion and to put our troops in greater danger."[10] According to this view, the legal framework for ensuring government transparency should be abandoned in order to protect American idealism against what might be perceived as its sordid reality. The utter weakness of this position has been cogently exposed by Greenwald. He writes:

> Think about what Obama's rationale would justify. Obama's claim—that release of the photographs "would be to further inflame anti-American opinion and to put our troops in greater danger"—means we should conceal or even outright lie about all the bad things we do that might reflect poorly on us. For instance, if an Obama bombing raid slaughters civilians in Afghanistan (as has happened several times already), then, by this reasoning, we ought to lie about what happened and conceal the evidence depicting what was done—as the Bush administration did—because release of such evidence "would be to further inflame anti-American opinion and to put our troops in greater danger."[11]

Indeed, according to this logic, the best way to deal with criminal behavior on the part of the American government is to suppress any evidence that it ever happened. Clearly, not only does this position shield executive wrongdoing on the part of the Bush administration, the CIA, and the national intelligence agencies, it also empties history of any critical meaning and ethical substance. How would history be written according to this logic? Would it seem reasonable in order to promote a sanitized view of history to eliminate images from textbooks and public view that record atrocities such as the lynchings of African Americans? When acts of state torture take place in prisons against people of color, should such criminal acts be disavowed on the grounds that they would discredit America's image in the eyes of its citizens and in the world? Would it be deemed patriotic to prevent young people from being able to see or study, for that matter, any disturbing image that might put into focus police brutality, the violence of the racial state, or orchestrated government terror often directed against the poor and minorities of race and class who are often considered disposable? Should the narrative of U.S. policies and politics be rewritten so as to cleanse it of human abuses, rights, and suffering in order to promote a cheerful Disney-like image of American society while simultaneously disclaiming any responsibility toward the other? Beyond suggesting that any critique of official power borders on being un-American, such an approach also would undermine the public's right to know about what its government, intelligence agencies, and military actually do, while at the same time discounting the American public's right to make ethical and political judgments about such actions as part of the democratic tradition of deliberation and participation.[12] It is difficult to view the suppression of America's wrongdoings as anything other than a form of bad faith politics that makes human rights not merely unthinkable but impossible to practice.

The task of governance and political leadership is not to bury dangerous memories but to draw out the darkness embedded in the recesses of the past and present, to make clear that the cover of secrecy and silence will not protect those who violate the law, and to reject a notion of national amnesia that sanctions illegality in the name of "moving forward," new watchwords that, significantly, no longer signal progress. But there is more at stake here than rewriting history in order to cleanse it of any wrongdoings: there is also an obligation of democratic leadership and governance. What is needed is public disclosure and a mode of government transparency that reveals that the United States has a long history of torture, one that extends from the genocide of Native Americans to the enslavement of millions of Africans and their descendants to the killing of 21,000 Vietnamese under the aegis of the CIA's infamous Phoenix Program. The purpose of this history is not to induce shame but to recognize that such crimes were legitimated by political conditions and institutionalized policies that must be excised from American domestic and foreign policies if there is to be hope for a future that does not simply repeat the past. History matters, not only because it allows society to uncover the hidden and, most recently, celebrated dimensions of cruelty but also because it points to the need for moral accountability that emerges out of self-reflection, dialogue, and debate.

What Obama misses in his refusal to make the crimes of the U.S. government public is the need for the American people to see what is wrong with such actions, who should be held accountable, why such acts of human cruelty should not happen again, and what actions must be taken to open up the possibilities for society to exercise collective judgments that enable a rejection of past actions as well as the possibility of a more just future. Moreover, as philosophy professor Maria Pia Lara argues, refusing to narrate human cruelty is tantamount to relinquishing the moral imperative to build a transformed democratic community. She contends that exposing and engaging the hidden dimensions of cruelty is part of a moral imperative "directed at making others understand that what happened did not need to happen." Moreover, such "stories [provide] us with a moral sense of the need to keep examining the past in order to ... build a space for self-reflection [and] define the process of establishing a connection between the collective critical examination of past catastrophes and the learning processes in which societies engage."[13]

At a time in history when American society is overly subject to the quasi-militarization of everyday life and endlessly exposed to mass-produced spectacles of commodified and ritualized violence, a culture of cruelty and barbarism becomes deeply entrenched and more easily tolerated. Beyond creating in this instance a moral and affective void in the collective consciousness—a refusal to recognize and rectify the illegal and morally repugnant violence, abuse, and suffering imposed on those alleged to be "disposable" others—such a culture contributes to the undoing of the very fabric of civilization and justice. The descent into barbarism can take many forms, but one version may be glimpsed when torture appears to be the only practice left that allows many Americans to feel alive, to mark what it means to be close to the register of death in a way that reminds them of the ability to feel within a culture that deadens every possibility of vitality. How else can we explain the fact that 49 percent of the American public "consider torture justified at least some of the time [and] fully 71 [percent] refuse to rule it out entirely"?[14] Clearly, such a culture is in dire need of being condemned, unlearned, and transformed through modes of critical education and public debate, if American democracy is to survive as more than a distant and unfulfilled promise. Americans have lived too long with governments that use power to promote violent acts, conveniently hiding their guilt behind a notion of secrecy and silence that selectively punishes those considered expendable—in its prisons, public schools, foster care institutions, and urban slums.

The Obama administration's refusal to release images of torture and abuse represents an attempt to determine what kinds of government action can be made visible and open to debate and what practices should be hidden from public purview, even if the government is guilty of war crimes. Sanctioning a legal system that operates in the service of abuse has more in common with dictatorships such as that in Pinochet's Chile, with its infamous torture chambers, world of night raids, and willingness to "disappear" all those considered enemies of the state, than it does with a vibrant and open democracy. Such secrecy shuts down public debate, makes the policies of governments invisible, and implies that state power should not be held accountable. But it does more. It sanctions criminal behavior as a virtue, undermines the need for public dialogue, contaminates moral values, and furthers a culture of violence and cruelty by suggesting that those who criminally promote torture, break the law, engage in human rights violations, and hurt children—in the interest of "protecting" citizens—should not be held responsible for their actions.

The state secrets privilege makes officially sanctioned power unaccountable, while also making a mockery of both citizenship and democracy itself. This practice is especially egregious coming from a U.S. president who campaigned on the need for government transparency and accountability. Government secrecy is the hallmark of authoritarian regimes, not substantive democracies, and critical citizenship does not prosper under such conditions. Obama has extended the Bush administration's abuse of the state secrets privilege by arguing that any lawsuits alleging government wrongdoing in the so-called war on terror should be dismissed in order to protect national security. As Bob Herbert puts it, "Lawyers from the Obama Justice Department have argued, as did lawyers from the Bush administration before them, that a lawsuit involving extraordinary rendition and allegations of extreme torture should be dismissed outright because discussions of such matters in court would harm national security. In other words, the victims, no matter how strong their case might be, no matter how badly they might have been abused, could never have their day in court."[15] The Bush and Obama view of the state secrets privilege effectively bars any real examination of such egregious violations. As human rights attorney David Cole argues with respect to the administration's stance,

> The bottom line is that executive wrongdoing in connection with the conflict with Al Qaeda should be shielded from judicial scrutiny. The administration has told courts that lawsuits challenging the Bush administration's warrantless wiretapping and extraordinary rendition programs must be dismissed because they involve "state secrets." On this theory, the executive can avoid any judicial review of criminal and unconstitutional wrongdoing simply by declaring its wrongs a secret.[16]

Equally upsetting is the fact that Obama has not only discouraged the formation of an independent commission to investigate acts of torture and abuse committed by the Bush administration but also refused to prosecute those who participated in such practices. Obama claims that "nothing will be gained by spending our time and energy laying blame for the past."[17] He asserts that for the good of the country, he does not want to look backward but forward, as if the past can be erased in order to produce a future that has any remnants of democratic ideals. Glenn Greenwald is right in asking the important question: "What kind of a country passes a law that has no purpose other than to empower its leader to suppress evidence of the torture it inflicted on people?"[18] Under Obama, justice has succumbed to the fog of national amnesia, falsifying any appeal to the future. It betrays the young people tortured by a criminal state that attempted to deny them any vestige of worth or rights; it continues to harm those young people who are imprisoned by the U.S. government and have had their futures stolen from them. Obama's call for reflection, rather than retribution, so constrains the possibility of reflection that it risks becoming a form of ignorance, a willful refusal to know. Reflection, if it is to be critical, deserves more from both Obama and the American public. As historian Cary Fraser has written:

> Maybe Obama's call for reflection may serve as a point of departure for American citizens to begin a campaign to save America from the miscalculations and hubris of its political and military leadership ... and recognize that the emergence of a culture of "permanent" war-preparedness within American life since 1945 constitutes a serious threat to American democracy—both as political theory and as institutions of governance.[19]

Against the wishes of the Obama administration, Attorney General Eric Holder appointed a special prosecutor, John Durham, to investigate the interrogation and abuse of prisoners by the CIA listed in the inspector general's 2004 report. Unfortunately, this is not a full-blown investigation of the crimes committed under the Bush administration and will not allow the inquiry to

> pursue the people who enabled those acts of torture—people like Secretary of Defense Donald Rumsfeld who personally instructed torturers in Afghanistan to "take the gloves off" in one case, or Assistant Attorney Generals John Yoo and Jay Bybee who ruled that anything short of the destruction of bodily organs or of a pain level equivalent to death was okay. Nor will [Obama] allow any investigation to look at acts

of torture that were authorized, like waterboarding, if they had the sanction of the Bush/Cheney White House.[20]

Holder's targeting of low-level interrogators while allowing high-level policymakers to go free replicates the disgraceful whitewashing of the Abu Ghraib prosecutions and also legitimates a two-tier system of justice in which "ordinary Americans are subjected to merciless punishment while the most powerful elites are vested with virtual immunity from the consequences of their lawbreaking."[21] This type of "accountability" bears a logic similar to that of the perpetrators of human rights violations and war crimes whose acts the criminal investigation is designed to expose. Obama's Department of Justice runs the risk of mimicking Bush's Department of Injustice by allowing to go free those who ordered or authorized torture and in some cases actually described in precise detail how the torture should be administered.

The lesson here is clear and morally repugnant. The powerful can trample civil liberties, ignore judicial safeguards, torture children, impose unspeakable abuses on detainees, participate in barbaric human rights violations, and be immune from prosecution. Obama's (un)reflectiveness and Holder's political cautiousness require us to ask more serious questions about how the cultures of war and cruelty "impose constraints on what can be heard, read, seen, felt, and known, and so work to undermine both a sensate understanding of war, and the conditions for a sensate opposition to war."[22] How and when did it become possible for a democratic country to ignore the suffering of children caused directly by state violence and, in doing so, dampen any sense of moral outrage, opposition, and critique while continuing to erase the lives of those most frail and unable to protect themselves, those whose lives are degraded, dehumanized, and discounted?[23] What does it mean when, in the name of democracy and freedom, a society uses doctors and other medical help to participate in the torture of children? In part, it means the illegalities that make such poisonous acts possible are not far removed from what the Nazis did in creating a culture in which doctors no longer saved human lives but were part of an army of medical warriors determined to use their professional skills to commit unspeakable acts in the name of racial purity. Instead of appealing to biological purity and racial hygiene, the U.S. government laid claim to waging a civilizational war that legitimated the conditions for members of the medical profession to become biological warriors in the service of torturing both adults and children—committing atrocious acts in the name of ideological and political purity. A nation devoted to a state of permanent war abroad and wedded to the punishing state at home cannot enlist its power and resources in the service of democracy.

Wedded to imperial ambitions and largely supportive of the national security state, the Obama administration can only offer high-sounding rhetoric and cosmetic adjustments to the Bush-Cheney approach to the war on terrorism, civil liberties, and torture. All the conditions that led to the torture of children under the Bush-Cheney regime are still in place under the Obama presidency. Greenwald gets it right in commenting on the failure of the Obama administration to deliver on its promise to uproot the legacy of the Bush-Cheney administration. He writes:

> The Obama administration has proven rather conclusively that tiny and cosmetic adjustments are the most it is willing to do. They love announcing new policies that cast the appearance of change but which have no effect whatsoever on presidential powers. With great fanfare, they announced the closing of CIA black sites—at a time when none was operating. They trumpeted the President's order that no interrogation tactics outside of the Army Field Manual could be used—at a time when approval for such tactics had been withdrawn. They repudiated the most extreme elements of

the Bush/Addington/Yoo "inherent power" theories—while maintaining alternative justifications to enable the same exact policies to proceed exactly as is. They flamboyantly touted the closing of Guantanamo—while aggressively defending the right to abduct people from around the world and then imprison them with no due process at Bagram. Their "changes" exist solely in theory—which isn't to say that they are all irrelevant, but it is to say that they change nothing in practice: i.e., in reality.[24]

One casualty of this political and moral indifference at the highest levels of government to a more just society and future are young people, especially those who become fodder for imperial adventures abroad and victims of the punishing state at home. Children, especially poor minority youth, have been punished for a long time in the United States. Removed from the inventory of social concerns and the list of cherished public assets, young people have been either disparaged as a symbol of danger or simply rendered invisible. Viewed as added casualties of the recession, youth are no longer included in a discourse about the promise of a better future. Instead, they are now considered part of a disposable population whose presence threatens to recall repressed collective memories of adult responsibility in the service of a social contract and democratic ideals. Injustice and inequality have a long legacy in the United States, and their most punishing modes and lethal effects have been largely directed against poor white and minority children. The shameful and willful state of American children—evident in what acclaimed novelist John Edgar Wideman calls "too many black boys in prison, too many black babies dying, too many hungry black youngsters being raised in dire poverty, too many terrible black schools," and too many homeless children—does not merely indicate neglect or an act of personal irresponsibility.[25] Personal responsibility matters, but it never tells the whole story or addresses problems for which it is neither responsible nor alone capable of changing.

What must be addressed are those larger social and political forces that speak to the unbearable hardening of a society that actively produces the needless suffering and death of its children. The moral nihilism of a market society, the move from a welfare state to a warfare state, the substitution of citizens for soldiers, the rampant racism of a "raceless" state, the collapse of education into training, and the rise of a pernicious corporate state make citizens immune to the suffering of others, especially children. As fear permeates the culture through ritualized spectacles of terror and a politics of state repression, representations of evil, often depicted as young and poor minorities, spread across the culture, circulated daily through reality TV shows such as *Cops, Speeders,* and *LAPD* and drama series such as *Southland.* Poor whites and minority youth, no longer useful for capital's profit margins, are largely portrayed as criminals, and every aspect of their behavior is both presented as a threat to the larger society and targeted as an object of disciplinary control. This in turn furthers a youth-control complex that serves to dehumanize them so as to make any abuse directed their way easy for the larger public to either ignore or applaud.[26] Such youth become "raw material for a growing corrections complex," and they also become the objects of the abuse and torture that is increasingly central to prison life.[27]

The ideology of hardness and cruelty runs through American culture like an electric current, sapping the strength of social relations and individual character, moral compassion, and collective action; offering up crimes against humanity that become fodder for video games and spectacularized media infotainment; and constructing a culture of cruelty that promotes a "symbiosis of suffering and spectacle."[28] As Chris Hedges argues,

Sadism is as much a part of popular culture as it is of corporate culture. It dominates pornography, runs ... through reality television and trash-talk programs and is at the core of the compliant, corporate collective. Corporatism is about crushing the capacity for moral choice. And it has its logical fruition in Abu Ghraib, the wars in Iraq and Afghanistan, and our lack of compassion for the homeless, our poor, the mentally ill, the unemployed and the sick.[29]

How else can we explain the lack of public interest or even a modicum of moral outrage over the news that the American government has abused and tortured the children of others as part of a war on terrorism? Or, for that matter, how can we explain the lack of moral outrage and political resistance to a government that is willing to torture children to get information—especially when that same government provides bailouts to those suspected of massive white-collar crimes, crimes that have produced unimaginable levels of hardship and suffering, and in such cases also "appears to believe that resort[ing] to grants of immunity to induce cooperation is more effective."[30] For example, Bernie Madoff's associates are encouraged by the U.S. government to provide information in exchange for immunity about where Madoff may have hidden billions. Meanwhile, children in U.S. custody as young as eleven years old are tortured for whatever information they might provide to military intelligence as part of fighting the war on terror. Truly, this type of logic is tantamount to a pact with the devil. And it is a logic that is reproduced endlessly in the dominant media. What is to be made of CNN posting a heart-wrenching and detailed story about a six-year-old boy kidnapped and brutally tortured by Al Qaeda operatives in Iraq, while refusing to acknowledge that the Bush administration also tortured children?[31] The moral outrage expressed in this story is more than deeply hypocritical: it also suggests the lack of civic courage, political integrity, and ethical values that has become characteristic of corporate-controlled media now reduced to being accomplices to corrupt government power. Even when a remarkable and courageous stand is taken in the media against torture, rarely is there a mention of those cases in which the U.S. government tortured children. For instance, on September 2, 2009, a fictional episode from the television series *Law and Order*, called "Memo from the Dark Side," aired a powerful and persuasive case against the Bush administration's use of the law to put policies in place that allowed the most horrendous crimes to take place. Focusing the story line around a character who clearly resembled attorney John Yoo, the episode was unsparing in its indictment of such lawyers; the man was portrayed as not only immoral, heartless, and cruel but also as a moral monster who violated a number of federal and international laws. Yet in spite of the political insight and moral courage displayed in this television episode, nothing was said about the actual torture of children, as if such horrendous crimes never happened. Even when torture is realistically confronted by creative television scriptwriters, the corporate media invariably establish a line that cannot be crossed—only so much of the dark side can be revealed.

Torture is a form of punishment and retaliation that destroys justice and defiles any pretense to democratic ideals. Once largely condemned, torture and the attendant culture of cruelty that makes it possible are no longer repudiated but actually enjoy public support by intellectuals, politicians, and the media. This situation becomes particularly indefensible and repugnant when children are tortured. Theodor Adorno once wrote in a different context that "all political instruction finally should be centered upon the idea that Auschwitz should never happen again. This would be possible only when it devotes itself openly, without fear of offending any authorities, to this most important of problems. To do this education must transform itself into sociology, that is, it must teach about the societal play of forces that operates beneath the surface of political forms."[32] Adorno's concern with the moral and political purposes of education is just as relevant today and applies to the issue of torture just as it once applied to the horrors of the Nazi concentration camp. In the aftermath of war with Nazi Germany, Adorno's response to retrograde ideologies and barbaric practices of state terrorism was to emphasize the role of critical agency and collective action. He saw this as the outcome of a moral and political project that defined education both in and out of schools as part of a broader civic mission to teach people how to be critical and autonomous and how to resist those ideologies, needs, social relations, and discourses that lead back to a politics where authority is simply obeyed and the totally administered society reproduces itself through a mixture of state force and orchestrated consensus. Adorno wanted to bring to light the horrors that gave rise to the Holocaust, and he searched for them in the play of social forces that lingered beneath the forms that enabled and sustained everyday life. He insisted on the need for an education that called injustice into question, was willing to resist the material and symbolic forces of domination, and refused to repeat the treachery of the past while engaging the possibilities of the future. Freedom in this instance meant being able to think critically and act courageously, even when confronted with the limits of one's knowledge.

There is a lesson here for both Obama and the American public. Surely, the Obama administration does not want to be seen as justifying policies and promoting conditions that result in the torture of children. Rather than forsake the past, Obama needs to interrogate it, mining its truths and making visible the forces and conditions that produced untold pain, suffering, and exploitation. Such an acknowledgment can only come to fruition if Obama moves away from his centrist policies and calls for radical economic, political, and educational changes in both how the United

States defines itself and how it uses power to expand and deepen democratic ideals, relations, and possibilities. As anger increasingly mounts among the American public over Obama's domestic and foreign policies, the Obama administration needs to take a long and hard look at what it has become and the conditions it is putting into place that suggest the United States is entering another and possibly more dangerous period in American history. What Adorno recognized in his time was that a slide into authoritarianism is not only a political and economic issue but also an educational one, and this is precisely the lesson that the Obama administration needs to remember. But at the same time, it is not simply up to Obama to make decisions about the future of American democracy. Such a task must be assumed collectively by an American public in full recognition that it has a choice about what kind of society it wants to be and what kind of future it wants to bequest to its children. Such a choice demands self-reflection, collective struggle, and embracing what it means to be attentive to one's own responsibility. Most of all, it means putting a premium on moral courage by offering individual and collective resistance to the dark forces of authoritarianism, increasingly camouflaged in lofty rhetoric advertising the domestic ideals of peace, freedom, and security. In the end, it may mean not abandoning the language of hope as the victory of theater over substance but reconfiguring the discourse of hope as part of a new space of opposition. Within such a space, a new type of struggle will take place in which various individuals, groups, and social movements come together to make a clean break from existing political parties and create a new oppositional party that takes seriously what it means to build a society in which democratic values, relations, and power suggest there is a politics after hope.

Notes

Foreword

1. Murray quotes in this and the next two paragraphs are from Daniel Tanoer, "Former UK Ambassador: CIA Sent People to Be 'Raped with Broken Bottles,'" *The Raw Story* (November 4, 2009), available online at http://rawstory.com/2009/2009/11/ambassador-cia-people-tortured/.

Preface and Acknowledgments

1. Heather Maher, "Majority of Americans Think Torture 'Sometimes' Justified," *CommonDreams.org* (December 4, 2009), available online at http://www.commondreams.org/headline/2009/12/04-0.
2. Hass cited in Sarah Pollock, "Robert Hass," *Mother Jones* (March–April 1992), p. 22.

Chapter One

1. George Orwell, *Nineteen Eighty-Four* (New York: Harcourt, Brace, 1949), p. 269.
2. I have taken up this issue in more detail in Henry A. Giroux, *Against the Terror of Neoliberalism* (Boulder, CO: Paradigm Publishers, 2008). See also Chris Hedges, *American Fascists: The Christian Right and the War on America* (New York: Free Press, 2006), and Sheldon S. Wolin, *Democracy Incorporated: Managed Democracy and the Specter of Inverted Totalitarianism* (Princeton, NJ: Princeton University Press, 2008).

3. For an excellent analysis of this issue, see Chris Hedges, *Empire of Illusion: The End of Literacy and the Triumph of Spectacle* (New York: Knopf Canada, 2009). See also George Monbiot, "The Triumph of Ignorance," *AlterNet* (October 31, 2008), available online at http://www.alternet.org/story/105447/the_triumph_ of_ignorance:_how_morons_succeed_in_u.s._politics/. For an extensive study of anti-intellectualism in America, see Richard Hoftstadter, *Anti-intellectualism in American Life* (New York: Vantage House, 1963), and Susan Jacoby, *The Age of American Unreason* (New York: Pantheon, 2008).

4. Zygmunt Bauman, *Wasted Lives: Modernity and Its Outcasts* (London: Polity Press, 2004), p. 131.

5. For the most extensive and exhaustive history on the technology of torture, see Darius Rejali, *Torture and Democracy* (Princeton, NJ: Princeton University Press, 2007). Some of the more instructive books on torture under the George W. Bush administration include Mark Danner, *Torture and Truth: America, Abu Ghraib, and the War on Terror* (New York: New York Review of Books, 2004); Jane Mayer, *The Dark Side: The Inside Story of How the War on Terror Turned into a War on American Ideals* (New York: Doubleday, 2008); and Phillipe Sands, *Torture Team* (London: Penguin, 2009). On the torture of children, see Michael Haas, *George W. Bush, War Criminal? The Bush Administration's Liability for 269 War Crimes* (Westport, CT: Praeger, 2009).

6. See Zygmunt Bauman, *Consuming Life* (London: Polity, 2007).

7. I take up these issues in Henry A. Giroux, *The University in Chains: Confronting the Military-Industrial-Academic Complex* (Boulder, CO: Paradigm Publishers, 2007).

8. The collapse of the social into the realm of the private has been the subject of a number of books. See, especially, C. Wright Mills's treatment of the issue in *The Sociological Imagination* (Oxford: Oxford University Press, 2000). See also Zygmunt Bauman, *In Search of Politics* (Stanford, CA: Stanford University Press, 1999), and Henry A. Giroux, *Public Spaces/Private Lives* (Lanham, MD: Rowman and Littlefield, 2003).

9. This term appears in the work of Zygmunt Bauman, who acknowledges that it was first used by John Dunn. See Bauman, *Consuming Life*, p. 140.

10. I take up the excesses of the Second Gilded Age in Henry A. Giroux, *The War on Youth: Democracy or Disposability?* (New York: Palgrave Macmillan, 2009).

11. Manifesto, *Left Turn: An Open Letter to U.S. Radicals* (New York: Fifteenth Street Manifesto Group, 2008), p. 19.

12. Ibid. See also Hedges, *Empire of Illusion,* and Henry A. Giroux, *Beyond the Spectacle of Terrorism* (Boulder, CO: Paradigm Publishers, 2006).

13. I take this issue up in great detail in Giroux, *Against the Terror of Neoliberalism.*

14. The best work being done on the politics of disposability can be found in Bauman, *Wasted Lives.*

15. Jean Comaroff, "Beyond Bare Life: AIDS, (Bio)Politics, and the Neoliberal Order," *Public Culture* 19, no. 1 (Winter 2007): 208.

16. Achille Mbembe, "Necropolitics," trans. Libby Meintjes, *Public Culture* 15, no. 1 (2003): 12.

17. Tanner Mirrlees, "Media Capitalism, the State, and 21st Century Media Democracy Struggles," *Relay* (April 26, 2009), available online at http://www.socialistproject.ca/relay/relay26_mcchesney.pdf.

18. Barbara Ehrenreich, "Is It Now a Crime to Be Poor?" *New York Times* (August 9, 2009), p. WK9.

19. David Bauder, "Fox's Glenn Beck: President Obama Is a Racist," *Associated Press* (July 28, 2009), available online at http://www.google.com/hostednews/ap/article/ALeqM5imGTdQH8JbOAWo_yKxNHpAMTCq_gD99NO3TG0.

20. Limbaugh quoted in Jeff Cohen and Steve Rendall, "Limbaugh a Color Man Who Has a Problem with Color?" *Fairness and Accuracy in Reporting* (June 6, 2000), available online at http://www.fair.org/index.php?page=2549.

21. Savage quoted in *Thinkers and Jokers* (July 2, 2007), available online at http://thinkersandjokers.com/thinker.php?id=2688.

22. Coulter quoted in Don Hazen, "The Tall Blonde Woman in the Short Skirt with the Big Mouth," *AlterNet* (June 6, 2006), available online at http://www.alternet.org/module/printversion/37162.

23. These quotes are taken from an excellent article by Eric Boehlert in which he criticizes the soft-peddling treatment that many in the press give to right-wing fanatics such as Michael Savage. See Boehlert, "The *New Yorker* Raises a Toast to Birther Nut Michael Savage," *Media Matters for America* (August 3, 2009), available online at http://mediamatters.org/print/columns/200908030038.

24. See Chris Hedges, "America the Illiterate," *Common-Dreams* (November 10, 2008), available online at http://www.commondreams.org/view/2008/11/10-6, and Terrence McNally, "How Anti-intellectualism Is Destroying America," *AlterNet* (August 15, 2008), available online at http://www.alternet.org/module/printversion/95109.

25. Judith Butler, *Frames of War: When Is Life Grievable?* (London: Verso, 2009).

26. For an excellent collection on military video games, see Nina B. Huntemann and Matthew Thomas Payne, eds., *Joystick Soldiers: The Politics of Play in Military Video Games* (New York: Routledge, 2010).

27. Arts and Entertainment, "Torture Will Just Have to Do," *Hamilton (Ontario) Spectator* (August 12, 2009), p. GO3.

28. Jane Mayer, "Whatever It Takes: The Politics of the Man behind *24*," *New Yorker* (February 26, 2007), p. 68.

29. Alessandra Stanley, "Suicide Bombers Strike, and America Is in Turmoil: Just Another Day in the Life of Jack Bauer," *New York Times* (January 12, 2007), p. B1.

30. See Butler, *Frames of War*. See also Slavoj Zizek, "The Depraved Heroes of *24* Are the Himmlers of Hollywood," *Guardian* (January 10, 2006), available online at http://www.guardian.co.uk/media/2006/jan/10/usnews.comment.

31. Faiz Shaker, "U.S. Military: Television Series '24' Is Promoting Torture in the Ranks," *Think Progress* (February 3, 2007), available online at http://thinkprogress.org/2007/02/13/torture-on-24/.

32. Hedges, *Empire of Illusion*, pp. 72–73.

33. Ibid., p. 10.

34. Eric Lichtblau, "Attacks on Homeless Bring Push on Hate Crime Laws," *New York Times* (August 8, 2009), p. A1.

35. National Coalition of the Homeless, *Hate, Violence, and Death on Main Street, 2008* (Washington, DC: National Coalition of the Homeless, 2009), p. 34, available online at http://www.nationalhomeless.org/publications/hatecrimes/hate_report_2008.pdf.

36. Lichtblau, "Attacks on Homeless."

37. National Coalition of the Homeless, *Hate, Violence, and Death on Main Street*.

38. Lichtblau, "Attacks on Homeless."

39. Mark Slouka, "Dehumanized: When Math and Science Rule the School," *Harper's Magazine* (September 5, 2009), p. 40.

40. Ibid.

41. Thomas C. Hilde, "Introduction," in *On Torture*, ed. Thomas C. Hilde (Baltimore, MD: Johns Hopkins University Press, 2008), p. 1.

42. Cheney quoted in Mayer, *Dark Side*, pp. 9–10.

43. Thomas C. Hilde, "Torture as a Greater Evil," in *On Torture*, ed. Hilde, p. 141.

44. Needless to say, the election of Barack Obama to the presidency has not prevented some individuals in the liberal media from refusing to use the word *torture*. For example, National Public Radio (NPR) ombudsman Alicia C. Shepard has attempted to defend NPR's decision to bar the use of *torture*. See Shepard, "Harsh Interrogations or Torture?" NPR (June 6, 2009), available online at http://www.npr.org/ombudsman/2009/06/harsh_interrogation_techniques.html. See also Glenn Greenwald's excellent response to this form of moral and political retreat from civic responsibility, "NPR's Ombudsman: Why We Bar the Word 'Torture,'" *Salon.com* (June 22, 2009), available online at http://www.salon.com/opinion/greenwald/2009/06/22/npr/.

45. Andrew Sullivan, "The Bigger Picture," *Daily Dish* (April 17, 2009), available online at http://andrewsullivan.theatlantic.com/the_daily_dish/2009/04/the-bigger-picture.html.

46. Tzvetan Todorov, *Torture and the War on Terror* (New York: Seagull Books, 2009), p. 39.

47. Ibid., p. 40.

48. Elaine Scarry, *The Body in Pain: The Making and Unmaking of the World* (New York: Oxford University Press, 1985), p. 56.

49. Ibid.

50. Todorov, *Torture and the War on Terror*, p. 60.

51. Mayer, *Dark Side*, p. 8.

52. Mark Danner, "US Torture: Voices from the Black Sites," *New York Review of Books* 56, no. 6 (April 9, 2009): 77.

Chapter Two

1. "Ronald Reagan on May 28, 1988, transmitting the Convention Against Torture to the Senate for ratification," cited in Glenn Greenwald, "America's Regression," *Salon* (December 4, 2009), available online at http://www.salon.com/opinion/greenwald/2009/12/03/torture.

2. Frank Rich, "The Banality of Bush White House Evil," *New York Times* (April 26, 2009), p. WK14.

3. The torture memos can be found at the American Civil Liberties Union Web site, http://www.aclu.org/safefree/general/olc_memos.html.

4. Andrew Sullivan, "The Bigger Picture," *Daily Dish* (April 17, 2009), available online at http://andrewsullivan.theatlantic.com/the_daily_dish/2009/04/the-bigger-picture.html.

5. Information on prisoners held at Guantánamo can be found in Andy Worthington, *The Guantanamo Files* (London: Pluto Press, 2007).

6. Ewen MacAskill, "Obama Releases Bush Torture Memos: Insects, Sleep Deprivation and Waterboarding among Approved Techniques by the Bush Administration," *Guardian* (April 16, 2009), available online at http://www.guardian.co.uk/world/2009/apr/16/torture-memos-bush-administration.

7. Ibid.

8. Andy Worthington, "Five Terrible Truths about the CIA Torture Memos," *Future of Freedom Foundation* (April 22, 2009), available online at http://www.commondreams.org/view/2009/04/22-6.

9. Editorial, "The Torturers' Manifesto," *New York Times* (April 19, 2009), p. WK9.

10. Ibid.

11. Bybee cited in Neil A. Lewis, "Official Defends Signing Interrogation Memos," *New York Times* (April 29, 2009), p. A12.

12. Thomas C. Hilde, "Torture as a Greater Evil," in *On Torture*, ed. Thomas C. Hilde (Baltimore, MD: Johns Hopkins University Press, 2008), p. 141. Unfortunately, the Department of Justice's Office of Professional Responsibility also ignored the Nuremberg judgment in its 2010 decision stating that Yoo and Bybee in authorizing torture had only committed "professional misconduct." An editorial in the *New York Times* asked, "Is this really the state of ethics in the American legal profession?" See "The Torture Lawyers," *New York Times* (February 24, 2010), p. A32.

13. This issue is taken up in Noam Chomsky, "American Amnesia: We Forget Our Atrocities Almost as Soon as We Commit Them," *TomDispatch.com* (May 20, 2009), available online at http://www.alternet.org/rights/140137/american_amnesia:_we_forget_our_atrocities_almost_as_soon_as_we_commit_them.

14. Scott Shane and Mark Mazzetti, "In Adopting Harsh Tactics, No Look at Past Use," *New York Times* (April 22, 2009), p. A1.

15. Chomsky, "American Amnesia."
16. Charles Kaiser, "Above the Fold: Know-Nothings at the *NYT*," *Columbia Journalism Review* (April 22, 2009), available online at http://www.cjr.org/campaign_desk/above_the_fold_knownothings_at.php.
17. Shane and Mazzetti, "In Adopting Harsh Tactics," p. A1.
18. Carl Boggs supplies an excellent commentary on the historical amnesia in the U.S. media surrounding the legacy of torture promoted by the United States. See Boggs, "Torture: An American Legacy," *CounterPunch.org* (June 17, 2009), available online at http://www.counterpunch.org/boggs06172009.html.
19. Ibid.
20. Ibid.
21. Many valuable sources document this history. Some exemplary texts include: A. J. Langguth, *Hidden Terrors: The Truth about U.S. Police Operations in Latin America* (New York: Pantheon Books, 1979); Gordon Thomas, *Journey into Madness: The True Story of Secret CIA Mind Control and Medical Abuse* (New York: Bantam, 1989); Mark Danner, *Torture and Truth: America, Abu Ghraib, and the War on Terror* (New York: New York Review of Books, 2004); Jennifer K. Harbury, *Truth, Torture, and the American Way: The History and Consequences of U.S. Involvement in Torture* (Boston: Beacon Press, 2005); Alfred McCoy, *A Question of Torture: CIA Interrogation, from the Cold War to the War on Terror* (New York: Metropolitan Books, 2006); and Darius Rejali, *Torture and Democracy* (Princeton, NJ: Princeton University Press, 2007). See also the more recent Jane Mayer, *The Dark Side: The Inside Story of How the War on Terror Turned into a War on American Ideals* (New York: Doubleday, 2008); and Phillipe Sands, *Torture Team* (London: Penguin, 2009).
22. Boggs, "Torture: An American Legacy."
23. Cited in Edward S. Herman, "Folks out There Have a 'Distaste of Western Civilization and Cultural Values,'" Center for Research on Globalization (September 15, 2001), available online at http://www.globalresearch.ca/articles/HER109A.html.
24. See, for example, Angela Y. Davis, *Abolition Democracy: Beyond Empire, Prisons, and Torture* (New York: Seven Stories Press, 2005), and Loic Wacquant, *Punishing the Poor* (Durham, NC: Duke University Press, 2009).
25. Ishmael Reed, "How Henry Louis Gates Got Ordained as the Nation's 'Leading Black Intellectual,'" *Black Agenda Report* (July

27, 2009), available online at http://www.blackagendareport
.com/?q=content/how-henry-louis-gates-got-ordained-nations-
leading-black-intellectual.

26. Pepe Lozano, "Chicago Torture Probe Draws Worldwide
Attention," *Political Affairs Magazine* (July 6, 2006), available online
at http://www.politicalaffairs.net/article/view/3770/1/196/.
See also Susan Saulny, "Ex-Officer Linked to Brutality Is Arrested," *New York Times* (October 22, 2008), available online
at http://www.nytimes.com/2008/10/22/us/22chicago
.html?partner=rssnyt&emc=rss.

27. Ibid. Also see John Conry's description of the torture that
took place in Chicago in what has been since called the John
Burge case. See John Conroy, *Unspeakable Acts, Ordinary People:
The Dynamics of Torture* (Berkeley: University of California Press,
2001).

28. Deborah Davis, "Torture Inc.: America's Brutal Prisons,"
Information Clearing House (March 28, 2005), available online
at http://www.informationclearinghouse.info/article8451
.htm.

29. See Brandon Keim, "Solitary Confinement: The Invisible
Torture," *Wired Science* (April 29, 2009), available online at http://
www.wired.com/wiredscience/2009/04/solitaryconfinement/.
See also Alexander Cockburn, "Torture: As American as Apple
Pie," *Free Press* (May 5, 2004), available online at http://www
.freepress.org/columns/display/2/2004/884. For a sustained
analysis of the various forms of human abuse in American
prisons, extending from extreme periods of solitary confinement
in supermax prisons to the use of electric shock and stun guns,
see Ruth Wilson Gilmore, *Golden Gulag: Prisons, Surplus, Crisis,
and Opposition in Globalizing California* (Berkeley: University of
California Press, 2007). See also A. Davis, *Abolition Democracy*,
and Loic Wacquant, "From Slavery to Mass Incarceration:
Rethinking the 'Race Question' in the U.S.," *New Left Review*
(January-February 2002): 41–60.

30. Keim, "Solitary Confinement."

31. Ibid.

32. Nina Bernstein, "Officials Hid Truth of Immigrant Deaths
in Jail," *New York Times* (January 10, 2010), p. A1.

33. Ibid.

34. Bob Herbert, "School to Prison Pipeline," *New York Times*
(June 9, 2007), p. A29.

35. Ibid.

36. Barbara Ehrenreich, "Is It Now a Crime to Be Poor?" *New York Times* (August 9, 2009), p. WK9.

37. Solomon Moore, "Mentally Ill Offenders Strain Juvenile System," *New York Times* (August 10, 2009), p. A1.

38. Ibid.

39. Ibid.

40. Randall R. Beger, "Expansion of Police Power in Public Schools and the Vanishing Rights of Students," *Social Justice* 29, no. 1 (2002): 120.

41. Greg Stohr, "Strip Search of Student Was Illegal, Top Court Says," *Bloomberg.com* (June 25, 2009), available online at http://www.bloomberg.com/apps/news?pid=20601087&sid=aKSsBXZ9Zb_8.

42. This term comes from David Garland, *The Culture of Control: Crime and Social Order in Contemporary Society* (Chicago: University of Chicago Press, 2002).

43. For an extensive treatment of zero-tolerance laws and the militarization of schools, see Christopher Robbins, *Expelling Hope: The Assault on Youth and the Militarization of Schooling* (Albany, NY: SUNY Press, 2008), and Kenneth Saltman and David Gabbard, eds., *Education as Enforcement: The Militarization and Corporatization of Schools* (New York: Routledge, 2003).

44. Victor M. Rios, "The Hypercriminalization of Black and Latino Male Youth in the Era of Mass Incarceration," in *Racializing Justice, Disenfranchising Lives,* ed. Ian Steinberg, Manning Marable, and Keesha Middlemass (New York: Palgrave, 2007), pp. 40–54.

45. For a superb analysis of urban marginality of youth in the United States and France, see Loic Wacquant, *Urban Outcasts* (London: Polity, 2008).

46. Advancement Project, in partnership with Padres and Jovenes Unidos, Southwest Youth Collaborative, *Education on Lockdown: The Schoolhouse to Jailhouse Track* (Chicago: Children and Family Justice Center of Northwestern University School of Law, March 24, 2005), pp. 17–18.

47. H. Snyder and M. Sickmund, *Juvenile Offenders and Victims: A National Report* (Washington, DC: Office of Juvenile Justice and Delinquency Prevention, 1995).

48. Children's Defense Fund, *America's Cradle to Prison Pipeline* (October 2007), available online at http://www.childrensdefense.org/helping-americas-children/cradle-to-prison-pipeline-campaign/. See also Equal Justice Initiative, *Cruel and*

Unusual: Sentencing 13- and 14-Year-Old Children to Die in Prison (November 2007), p. 77, available online at http://www.eji.org/eji/files/20071017cruelandunusual.pdf.

49. Cited in Evelyn Nieves, "California Proposal Toughens Penalties for Young Criminals," *New York Times* (March 6, 2000), pp. A1, A15.

50. Barry Feld, "Criminalizing the American Juvenile Court," *Crime and Justice* 17 (1993): 251.

51. U.S. Department of Justice, *Report: Investigation of the Lansing Residential Center, Louis Gossett, Jr. Residential Center, Tryon Residential Center, and Tryon Girls Center* (Washington, DC: U.S. Government, 2009), available online at http://www.usdoj.gov/crt/split/documents/NY_juvenile_facilities_findlet_08-14-2009.pdf.

52. Nicholas Confessore, "4 Youth Prisons in New York Used Excessive Force," *New York Times* (August 25, 2009), p. A1.

53. U.S. Department of Justice, *Report: Investigation of the Lansing Residential Center.*

54. Ibid.

55. Seth Mydans, "Torture and Death in Cambodian Prison Are Recounted at Trial," *New York Times* (July 15, 2009), p. A4.

56. Ibid.

57. Roy Eidelson, "How Americans Came to Support Torture, in Five Steps," *Alternet* (December 6, 2009), available online at www.alternet.org/story/139993.

Chapter Three

1. Jonathan Schell, "Torture and Truth," *Nation* (June 15, 2009), p. 17.

2. One egregious example of a Guantánamo detainee being brutalized into producing a false confession came to light in October 2009. Federal court judge Colleen Kollar-Kotelly denounced the U.S. government for torturing Fouad al-Rabiah and soliciting a confession that she described as not believable. Al-Rabiah, a Kuwaiti citizen, had been held at Guantánamo since 2002 and claimed that he repeatedly told his interrogators what they wanted to hear in order to stop the abuse he had to endure from them, including the "frequent flyer program" and threats of rendition to another country to be tortured. Judge Kollar-Kotelly dismissed the

confessions, chided the government for using them, and ordered the release of al-Rabiah. This story is fully explored in Andy Worthington, "Judge Confirms Detainee Tortured to Make False Confessions," *Truthout.org* (October 14, 2009), available online at http://www.truthout.org/10140910. The judge's opinion can be found at http://documents.propublica .org/guantanamo-detainee-fouad-mahmoud-al-rabiah-s-petition-for-habeus-corpus#p=1.

3. Pilar Calveiro, "Torture's New Methods and Meanings," in *On Torture*, ed. Thomas C. Hilde (Baltimore, MD: Johns Hopkins University Press, 2008), p. 120.

4. International Committee of the Red Cross, *ICRC Report on the Treatment of Fourteen "High Value" Detainees in CIA Custody* (Washington, DC: International Committee of the Red Cross, 2007), pp. 7–8.

5. Warren Richey, "Despite Warnings, Officials Used 43 Months of Severe Isolation to Force Jose Padilla to Tell All He Knew about Al Qaeda," *Christian Science Monitor* (August 14, 2007), available online at http://www.csmonitor.com/2007/0814/p11s01-usju.htm?print=true.

6. Schell, "Torture and Truth," p. 16.

7. Ibid.

8. Cheney quoted in Jane Mayer, *The Dark Side: The Inside Story of How the War on Terror Turned into a War on American Ideals* (New York: Doubleday, 2008), pp. 9–10.

9. Mark Danner, "The Red Cross Torture Report: What It Means," *New York Review of Books* 56, no. 7 (April 30, 2009): 48.

10. Ibid.

11. George W. Bush, "Statement by the President—United Nations International Day in Support of Victims of Torture," *Office of the Press Secretary—The White House* (June 26, 2002), available online at http://web.archive.org/web/20030820132648/www .whitehouse.gov/news/releases/2003/06/20030626-3.html.

12. Michelle Shepard, *Guantanamo's Child* (New York: John Wiley, 2008), p. 94.

13. Ibid., p. 95.

14. Ibid., pp. 94–95.

15. See the May 30, 2005, Stephen Bradbury, Office of Legal Council, memo, available online at http://s3.amazonaws.com/ propublica/assets/missing_memos/28OLCmemofinalredact30 May05.pdf.

16. Bush, "Statement by the President."

17. All of these incidents can be found in the Office of the Inspector General, *Special Review: Counterterrorism Detention and Interrogation Activities September 2001–October 2003* (May 7, 2004), available online at http://luxmedia.vo.llnwd.net/o10/clients/aclu/IG_Report.pdf. See also Glenn Greenwald, "What Every American Should Be Made to Learn about the IG Torture Report," *Salon.com* (August 24, 2009), available online at http://www.salon.com/opinion/greenwald/2009/08/24/ig_report/print.html.

18. Dave Lindorff, "Getting Away with Torture," *CounterPunch* (August 26, 2009), available online at www.counterpunch.org/lindorff08262009.html.

19. Thomas C. Hilde, "Torture as a Greater Evil," in *On Torture*, ed. Hilde, p. 141.

20. Luke Mitchell, "We Still Torture: The New Evidence from Guantánamo," *Harper's Magazine* (July, 2009), pp. 49–50.

21. Phillipe Sands cited in Bill Moyer, "Welcome to the Journal," *Bill Moyer Journal* (May 9, 2008), available online at http://www.pbs.org/moyers/journal/05092008/transcript.html.

22. Sands, cited in ibid.

23. Calveiro, "Torture's New Methods and Meanings," p. 122.

24. Darius Rejali, *Torture and Democracy* (Princeton, NJ: Princeton University Press, 2007), esp. pp. 259–401.

25. See Theodor Adorno, "Education after Auschwitz," in his *Critical Models: Interventions and Catchwords* (New York: Columbia University Press, 1998), p. 194.

26. Cited in Philip Watts, "Bush Advisor Says President Has Legal Power to Torture Children," *Information Clearing House* (January 8, 2006), available online at http://www.informationclearinghouse.info/article11488.htm.

27. Jess Braven and Gary Fields, "How Do U.S. Interrogators Make a Captured Terrorist Talk? *Wall Street Journal* (March 4, 2003), p. B1.

28. Cited in Rebecca Lemov, "The American Science of Interrogation," *Los Angeles Times* (October 22, 2005), available online at http://condition.org/lat5a22.htm.

29. Danner, "Red Cross Torture Report," p. 51.

30. Deborah Solomon, "Global Warning: Questions for James Inhofe," *New York Times* (November 29, 2009), p. MM16.

31. Ibid.

32. Deborah Solomon, "Power of Attorney: Questions for John Yoo," *New York Times* (January 3, 2010), p. MM15.

33. Ibid.

34. Judith Butler, *Frames of War: When Is Life Grievable?* (Brooklyn, NY: Verso, 2009), p. 3.

Chapter Four

1. Agence France-Presse, "Cheney Says Detainees Are Well Treated," *New York Times* (June 24, 2005), available online at http://www.nytimes.com/2005/06/24/politics/24cheney .html?pagewanted=print.

2. Three reports are especially useful on this matter. See Laurel E. Fletcher and Eric Stover, *Guantánamo and Its Aftermath: U.S. Detention and Interrogation Practices and Their Impact on Former Detainees* (Berkeley, CA: Human Rights Center and International Human Rights Law Clinic, 2008), available online at http://ccrjustice.org/files/Report_GTMO_ And_Its_Aftermath.pdf; International Committee of the Red Cross, *ICRC Report on the Treatment of Fourteen "High Value" Detainees in CIA Custody* (Washington, DC: International Committee of the Red Cross, 2007), pp. 1–30; and Center for Constitutional Rights, *Report on Torture and Cruel, Inhuman, and Degrading Treatment of Prisoners at Guantánamo Bay, Cuba* (Washington, DC: Center for Constitutional Rights, 2006), available online at http://ccrjustice.org/files/ Report_ReportOnTorture.pdf.

3. Glenn Greenwald, "Mohammed Jawad and Obama's Efforts to Suspend Military Commissions," *Salon.com* (January 21, 2009), available online at http://www.salon.com/opinion/ greenwald/2009/01/21/Guantánamo/.

4. Scott Horton, "The Guantanamo 'Suicides': A Camp Delta Sergeant Blows the Whistle," *Harper's Magazine* (January 18, 2010), available online at http://harpers.org/archive/2010/01/ hbc-90006368.

5. Ibid.

6. Ibid.

7. Center for Constitutional Rights, *Report on Torture.*

8. Ibid.

9. Ibid.

10. Ibid.
11. Fletcher and Stover, *Guantánamo and Its Aftermath.*
12. Center for Constitutional Rights, *Report on Torture.*
13. Ibid.
14. International Committee of the Red Cross, *ICRC Report on the Treatment of Fourteen "High Value" Detainees,* p. 10.
15. Paisley Dodds, "Guantánamo Bay: Female Interrogators' Aired," *Seattle Times* (January 28, 2005), available online at http://seattletimes.nwsource.com/html/nationworld/2002162977_gitmo28.html.
16. Luke Mitchell, "We Still Torture: The New Evidence from Guantánamo," *Harper's Magazine* (July 2009), pp. 49–55.
17. See Jason Leopold, "Blistering Indictment Leveled against Obama over His Handling of Bush-Era Crimes," *Truthout* (December 12, 2009), available online at www.truthout.org/12110911?print.
18. Associated Press, "Bagram Detainees Stage Protest against US Treatment," *CommonDreams.Org* (July 16, 2009), available online at http://www.commondreams.org/headline/2009/07/16-0.
19. Petra Bartosiewicz, "A Thousand Little Gitmos," *Mother Jones* (August 17, 2009), available online at http://www.motherjones.com/politics/2009/07/thousand-little-gitmos.
20. Ibid.
21. Ibid.
22. Ibid.
23. Ibid.
24. The great tragedy of American politics reveals itself not only in the defense of torture by a discredited former vice president, Dick Cheney, but also among many members of the Republican Party and in newspapers as reputable as the *Washington Post.* The notion that torture is justifiable if it works to secure information is a morally bankrupt argument in any aspiring democracy. As Tom Parker, policy director for counterterrorism and human rights at Amnesty International, contends, "Democratic societies don't use torture under any circumstances. It is illegal and immoral." Parker is cited in Susie Madrak, "If Torture Works, That Makes It Okay? What a Morally Bankrupt Argument," *Crooks and Liars* (August 29, 2009), available online at http://crooksand liars.com/30825/print. Of course, even the pragmatic argument about torture has been repudiated by former FBI interrogator

Ali H. Soufan. See Soufan, "What Torture Never Told Us," *New York Times* (September 6, 2009), p. WK9.

Chapter Five

1. Warren Sack, "Agnostics: A Language Game," in *Making Things Public,* ed. Bruno Latour and Peter Weibel (Cambridge, MA: MIT Press, 2005), p. 966.

2. Peter Beilharz, *Zygmunt Bauman: Dialect of Modernity* (London: Sage, 2000), p. 158.

3. Mark Reinhardt and Holly Edwards, "Traffic in Pain," in *Beautiful Suffering: Photography and the Traffic in Pain,* ed. Mark Reinhardt, Holly Edwards, and Erina Duganne (Chicago: University of Chicago Press, 2006), p. 7.

4. These ideas are taken from Zygmunt Bauman, *Consuming Life* (London: Polity, 2007), pp. 126–128.

5. See, for example, Rahul Mahajan, "We Think the Price Is Worth It," *Fair and Accuracy in Reporting* (November-December 2001), available online at http://www.fair.org/index.php?page=1084.

6. Ibid.

7. Michael Haas, "Children, Unlamented Victims of Bush War Crimes," *FactPlatform* (May 4, 2009), available online at http://www.factjo.com/Manbar_En/MemberDetails.aspx?Id=187.

8. Sherwood Ross, "Iraqi Children in US Prisons," *Political Affairs Magazine* (November 9, 2008), available online at http://www.politicalaffairs.net/article/articleview/7704/.

9. Ralph Lopez, "President Carter: Many Children Were Tortured under Bush," *Truthout.org* (July 22, 2009), available online at http://www.truthout.org/080309X?n.

10. Ibid.

11. Cited in Alex Koppelman, "Hersh: Children Sodomized at Abu Ghraib, on Tape," *Salon* (July 15, 2004), available online at http://www.salon.com/politics/war_room/2004/07/15/hersh/.

12. "Further Iraqi Abuse Claims Hit US," *Telegraph* (May 21, 2004), available online at http://www.telegraph.co.uk/news/1462455/Further-Iraqi-abuse-claims-hit-US.html.

13. Cited in Thomas Ruetter's documentary *Iraq: One More Sin—Evidence of Children Being Abused in Abu Ghraib.* The television broadcast was aired on Global Network in Germany on July

5, 2004. A copy of the transcript in English is available online at http://carryabigsticker.com/news/iraq_child_prisoners.htm.
14. Quoted in ibid.
15. Jonathan Steele, "Inmates Tell of Sexual Abuse and Beatings in Iraq's Overcrowded Juvenile Prison System," *Guardian* (September 8, 2008), available online at http://www.guardian.co.uk/world/2008/sep/08/iraq.humanrights.
16. Ibid.
17. Michael Haas, *George W. Bush, War Criminal? The Bush Administration's Liability for 269 War Crimes* (Santa Barbara, CA: Greenwood Books, 2009).
18. Ibid., esp. pp. 155–164, 196.
19. Haas, "Children, Unlamented Victims."
20. "US Detains Children at Guantánamo Bay," *Guardian* (April 23, 2003), available online at http://www.guardian.co.uk/world/2003/apr/23/usa.
21. Ibid.
22. Both comments are quoted in Andy Worthington, "Omar Khadr: The Guantánamo Files," *Future of Freedom Foundation* (October 20, 2008), available online at http://www.fff.org/comment/com0810k.asp. See also Worthington's excellent book *The Guantánamo Files: The Stories of the 774 Detainees in America's Illegal Prisons* (London: Pluto Press, 2007).
23. Quoted in Andy Worthington, "The Case of Mohamed Jawad," *CounterPunch.org* (October 17, 2007), available online at http://www.counterpunch.org/worthington1017200.html.
24. ACLU, "Amended Petition for Writ of Habeas Corpus on Behalf of Mohammed Jawad," June 2009, available online at http://www.aclu.org/pdfs/natsec/amended_jawad_2009113.pdf.
25. Haas, *George W. Bush, War Criminal?* p. 157.
26. Cori Crider, "Guantánamo Children," *Guardian* (July 19, 2008), available online at http://www.guardian.co.uk/world/2008/jul/19/humanrights.usa.
27. Haas, *George W. Bush, War Criminal?* pp.155–156.
28. See International Committee of the Red Cross, *Report of the International Committee of the Red Cross (ICRC) on the Treatment by the Coalition Forces of Prisoners of War and Other Persons Protected by the Geneva Conventions in Iraq during Arrest, Internment and Interrogation* (February 2004), available online at http://www.informationclearinghouse.info/pdf/icrc_iraq.pdf.
29. Ibid. See also Rajiv Chandrasekaran and Scott Wilson, "Mistreatment of Detainees Went beyond Guards' Abuse—

Ex-Prisoners, Red Cross Cite Flawed Arrests, Denial of Rights," *Washington Post* (May 11, 2004), p. A01.

30. Neil A. Lewis, "Some Held at Guantánamo Are Minors, Lawyers Say," *New York Times* (June 13, 2005), available online at http://www.nytimes.com/2005/06/13/politics/13gitmo.html.

31. For a riveting, compassionate, and exhaustive analysis of the Omar Khadr case, see Michelle Shepard, *Guantánamo's Child: The Untold Story of Omar Khadr* (New York: John Wiley and Sons, 2008).

32. Richard J. Wilson, "Children in Armed Conflict: The Detention of Children at Guantánamo Bay, and the Trial for War Crimes by Military Commission of Omar Khadr, a Child," *Social Science Social Network* Washington College of Law Research Paper no. 2009-13, February 2009, available online at http://papers.ssrn.com/sol3/papers.cfm?abstract_id=1368323.

33. Amnesty International, *Document—USA: In Whose Best Interests? Omar Khadr, Child "Enemy Combatant," Facing Military Commission* (New York: Amnesty International, 2008), available online at http://www.amnesty.org/en/library/info/AMR51/028/2008/en.

34. Ibid.

35. Warren Richey, "US Gov't Broke Padilla through Intense Isolation, Say Experts"(August 14, 2007), available online at http://www.csmonitor.com/2007/0814/p11s01-usju.html.

36. Haas, "Children, Unlamented Victims."

37. Wilson, "Children in Armed Conflict."

38. Amnesty International, *Document—USA.*

39. Steve Hynd, "Judge Orders Gitmo Detainee, Held since Age 14, Freed," *Crooks and Liars* (January 15, 2009), available online at http://crooksandliars.com/node/25259/print.

40. ACLU Petition for Writ of Habeas Corpus, "Amended Petition for Writ of Habeas Corpus on Behalf of Mohammed Jawad," June 2009, available online at http://www.aclu.org/pdfs/natsec/amended_jawad_2009113.pdf.

41. Quoted in Worthington, "Case of Mohamed Jawad."

42. William Glaberson, "Government Might Allow U.S. Trial for Detainee," *New York Times* (July 25, 2009), p. A14.

43. ACLU, "Mohammed Jawad—Habeas Corpus," *Safe and Free* (January 13, 2009), available online at http://www.aclu.org/safefree/detention/38714res20090113.html.

44. ACLU, "Amended Petition."

45. Ibid.

46. Ibid.

47. Glenn Greenwald, "Mohammed Jawad and Obama's Efforts to Suspend Military Commissions," *Salon.com* (January 21, 2009), available online at http://www.salon.com/opinion/greenwald/2009/01/21/Guantánamo/.

48. Bob Herbert, "How Long Is Enough?" *New York Times* (June 30, 2009), p. A21.

49. Colonel Vandeveld's sworn affidavit is included in ACLU, "Amended Petition."

50. Ibid.

51. Amnesty International, *United States of America—From Ill-Treatment to Unfair Trial: The Case of Mohammed Jawad, Child "Enemy Combatant"* (London: Amnesty International, 2008), pp. 12–13.

52. ACLU, "Amended Petition."

53. Meteor Blades, "Army Psychologist Pleads 'Fifth' in Case of Prisoner 900," *DailyKos* (August 14, 2008), available online at http://www.dailykos.com/story/2008/8/14/202414/685/395/568118.

54. Ibid.

55. Colonel Vandeveld's sworn affidavit is included in ACLU, "Amended Petition."

56. Amnesty International, *United States of America*, p. 20.

57. ACLU, "Amended Petition."

58. Amnesty International, *United States of America*, p. 31.

59. Ibid.

60. ACLU, "Amended Petition."

61. Quoted in Jason Leopold, "Obama Administration Cooks up New Legal Argument for Detaining Guantánamo Prisoner," *Truthout.org* (July 28, 2009), available online at http://www.truthout.org/072809.

62. Valtin, "'So Ordered': U.S. to Release Mohammed Jawad after Six Years of False Imprisonment," *Daily Kos* (July 30, 2009), available online at http://www.dailykos.com/story/2009/7/30/18119/5521.

63. William Glaberson, "Judge Orders Release of Young Detainee at Guantánamo," *New York Times* (July 31, 2009), p. A14.

64. Associated Press, "Young Guantánamo Prisoner Back in Afghanistan," *New York Times* (August 24, 2009), available online at http://www.nytimes.com/aponline/2009/08/24/world/AP-CB-Guantánamo-Prisoner-Release.html?scp=3&sq=Mohammed%20Jawad&st=cse.

65. Cited in Daphine Eviatar, "Military Lawyer Claims US Paid

Guantánamo Prosecution Witnesses," *Washington Independent* (August 5, 2009), available online at http://washingtonindependent .com/53655/gitmo-detainee-claims-u-s-paid-prosecution-witnesses.

66. Even so-called liberals cannot give up the fallacy of the "ticking time bomb" theory. With the arrest of Najibullah Zazi, the alleged mastermind of a bomb plot, Michael Crowley, a writer for the *New Republic*, not only suggested that this case resembled the ticking time bomb scenario but also asserted that such a scenario raised the issue of whether torture might be justified in this instance. As he put it, referring to federal agents, "How hard should they be working him?" Indeed, Crowley seemed to be asking, Why bother with the moral violations and illegal practices that such practices suggest? See Crowley, "The Ticking Zazi Bomb," *New Republic* (September 25, 2009), available online at http://www.tnr.com/blog/the-plank/the-ticking-zazi-bomb.

67. As recently as July 22, 2009, the *New York Times* ran a story suggesting that Attorney General Eric H. Holder should not appoint a prosecutor to investigate the use of interrogations that tortured people, the reason being that he runs the risk of alienating the White House, which has more important policies to promote, and the Central Intelligence Agency, which would feel betrayed. See David Johnston, "For Holder, Inquiry on Interrogation Poses Tough Choice," *New York Times* (July 22, 2009), p. A15. In this instance, political expediency trumps both ethics and human decency.

68. MSNBC, *Hardball with Chris Matthews*, transcript (May 20, 2009), available online at http://www.votesmart .org/speech_detail.php?sc_id=462234&keyword=&phrase=&contain= ?q=print.

69. Darius Rejali, *Torture and Democracy* (Princeton, NJ: Princeton University Press, 2007), p. xv.

70. Paul Steinhauser, "Poll: Don't Investigate Torture Techniques," *CNN Political Ticker* (May 6, 2009), available online at http://politicalticker.blogs.cnn.com/2009/05/06/poll-don't-investigate-torture-techniques/.

71. Glenn Greenwald, "The Neda Video, Torture, and the Truth-Revealing Power of Images," *Salon.com* (June 24, 2009), available online at http://www.commondreams.org/views/2009/06/24-10.

72. Andrew Sullivan, "Is the US Now a Non-Geneva State?" *Daily Dish* (April 28, 2008), available online at http://andrewsullivan.theatlantic.com/the_daily_dish/2008/04/is-the-us-now-a.html.

Chapter Six

1. Zygmunt Bauman, *The Individualized Society* (London: Polity, 2001), pp. 54–55.

2. John Brenkman, *The Cultural Contradictions of Democracy: Political Thought since September 11* (Princeton, NJ: Princeton University Press, 2007), p. 12.

3. Stanley Aronowitz, "Let's Break from the Party of War and Wall Street," ZNet (January 11, 2010), available online at http://www.zmag.org/znet/viewArticle/23601.

4. Barack Obama, "Obama's Address on the War on Afghanistan," *New York Times* (December 1, 2009), available online at http://www.nytimes.com/2009/12/02/world/asia/02prexy.text.html?_r=1&pagewanted=all.

5. Adam Liptak, "Obama Administration Weighs in on State Secrets, Raising Concern on the Left," *New York Times* (August 4, 2009), p. A11.

6. Glenn Greenwald, "Defeat of Graham-Lieberman and the Ongoing War on Transparency," *Salon.com* (June 9, 2009), available online at http://www.salon.com/opinion/greenwald/2009/06/09/transparency.

7. Ibid.

8. Adam Serwer, "No Human Rights Fiction?" *Tapped—The American Prospect* (December 2, 2009), available online at http://www.prospect.org/csnc/blogs/tapped_archive?month=12&year=2009&base_name=no_human_rights_fiction.

9. Butler, *Frames of War: When Is Life Grievable?* (London: Verso, 2009), p. 74.

10. Scott Wilson, "Obama Shifts on Abuse Photos," *Washington Post* (May 14, 2009), available online at http://mobile.washingtonpost.com/detail.jsp?key=387026&rc=wo&npc=wo.

11. Greenwald, "Defeat of the Graham-Lieberman."

12. On this issue, see Butler, *Frames of War,* esp. pp. 39–40.

13. Maria Pia Lara, *Narrating Evil: A Postmetaphysical Theory*

of Reflective Judgment (New York: Columbia University Press, 2007), pp. 14–16, 19.

14. Roy Eidelson, "How Americans Think about Torture—and Why," *TruthOut.org* (May 11, 2009), available online at http://www.truthout.org/051209c.

15. Bob Herbert, "Who Are We?" *New York Times* (June 23, 2009), p. A25.

16. David Cole, "Bush Law Continued," *Nation* (April 6, 2009), p. 8.

17. Obama quoted in Mark Mazzetti and Scott Shane, "Interrogation Memos Detail Harsh Tactics by the CIA," *New York Times* (April 16, 2009), p. A1.

18. Glenn Greenwald, "Obama's Support for the New Graham-Lieberman Secrecy Law," *Salon.com* (June 1, 2009), available online at http://www.salon.com/opinion/greenwald/2009/06/01/photos/index.html.

19. Cary Fraser, "Terror, Torture and Tyranny," *Trinidad and Tobago Review* (May 4, 2009), available online at http://www.tntreview.com/?p=490.

20. Dave Lindorff, "Getting Away With Torture," *Counter-Punch.org* (August 26, 2009), available online at http://www.counterpunch.org/lindorff08262009.html.

21. Glenn Greenwald, "Eric Holder Announces Investigation Based on Abu Ghraib Model," *Salon.com* (August 24, 2009), available online at http://www.salon.com/opinion/greenwald/2009/08/24/holder/print.html.

22. Butler, *Frames of War*, p. 100.

23. I have paraphrased Judith Butler in this sentence. See ibid., p. 77.

24. Glenn Greenwald, "Victory on Preventive Detention Law: In Context," *Salon.com* (September 24, 2009), available online at http://www.salon.com/opinion/greenwald/2009/09/24/detention/print.html.

25. John Edgar Wideman, "Fatheralong," *Harper's Magazine* (August 2009), p. 9.

26. I take up this issue in great detail in Henry A. Giroux, *Youth in a Suspect Society: Democracy or Disposability?* (New York: Palgrave Macmillan, 2009).

27. Christian Parenti, *Lockdown America: Police and Prisons in the Age of Crisis* (London: Verso, 1999), p. 137.

28. Mark Reinhardt and Holly Edwards, "Traffic in Pain," in *Beautiful Suffering: Photography and the Traffic in Pain*, ed.

Mark Reinhardt, Holly Edwards, and Erina Duganne (Chicago: University of Chicago Press, 2006), p. 9.

29. Chris Hedges, "America Is in Need of Moral Bailout," *Truthdig.com* (March 23, 2009), available online at http://www.truthdig.com/report/item/20090323_america_is_in_need_of_a_moral_bailout/.

30. This quote comes from a personal correspondence with Professor Thomas Goetzl on August 3, 2009.

31. See Anwa Damon, "Terrorists Kidnap, Torture Boy to Bully Iraqi Policeman," *CNN.com* (August 7, 2009), available online at http://www.cnn.com/2009/WORLD/meast/08/07/iraq.kidnapped.boy/index.html.

32. Adorno's essay was first presented as a radio lecture on April 18, 1966, under the title "Padagogik nack Auschwitz." The first published version appeared in 1967. The English translation appears in Theodor Adorno, "Education after Auschwitz," in his *Critical Models: Interventions and Catchwords* (New York: Columbia University Press, 1998), p. 203.

◆

Index

Abu Ghraib prison: bad apple argument at, 19–20; children detained in, 61–63; deaths at, xxii, xxiii; photos of detainee abuse in, xxxii, 40; prosecutions of abuse at, 94
Accountability for past deeds, 60–61, 89–91, 92–93
ACLU (American Civil Liberties Union), xvi, xxiv, 26
Adorno, Theodor, 41, 99–100, 101
Afghanistan: Bagram air base, 53, 74–75; children detained in, 66–67; detainees murdered in custody in, xxiii–xxiv; Kandahar detention facility, statement of interpreter at, xiii–xiv; photos of detainee abuse in, 86–91
Albright, Madeleine, 60
Ali, Omar, 63
American Civil Liberties Union (ACLU), xvi, xxiv, 26
Authoritarianism: American, defining elements of, 54–55, 81–82; emergence of, 4, 101; secrecy and, 91–92

Bad apple argument, 19–20
Bartosiewicz, Petra, 53–54
Bauman, Zygmunt, 2, 3

Baz, Suhaib Badr-Addin al-, 63
Beatings and physical abuse, 50–51
Beck, Glenn, 8
Beger, Randall, 28
Beilharz, Peter, 57–58
Bensayah, Belkacem, 48–49
Bernstein, Nina, 26
Black, Cofer, 35–36
Black sites: Bush administration and, 16, 33, 36; at Guantánamo Bay, 48; Obama administration and, xi, 84, 95; in Uzbekistan, x
Blades, Meteor, 75
Bodies, disappearing, 47–55
Boggs, Carl, 23, 24
Boumediene, Lakhadar, 50–51
Bradbury, Steven, 20, 21
The Brave One (movie), 9–10
Braven, Jess, 42–43
"Bum fight" videos, 12–13
Burge, Jon, 25
Burney, Charles, 35
Bush, George W., 1–2, 36
Bush administration: after September 11, 14–17, 36; as authoritarian, 81–82; corruption of, 45; culture of cruelty and, 5–6, 45–46; culture of war and, xxx–xxxi; as eager to show off, 39;

125

◆

About the Author

Henry A. Giroux holds the Global TV Network Chair in English and Cultural Studies at McMaster University in Canada. His most recent books include *The University in Chains: Confronting the Military-Industrial-Academic Complex* (2007), *Against the Terror of Neoliberalism: Politics Beyond the Age of Greed* (2008), and *Youth in a Suspect Society: Democracy or Disposability?* (2009).